Theo's Tricks

And other Greek Yarns

By William E. Tudor

Theo's Tricks

© Copyright 2013 William E. Tudor

All rights reserved. No part of this publication may be reproduced in any form or by any means, electronic or mechanical, including photocopying, recording, or any other information storage and retrieval system, without the written permission of the publisher.

Printed in the United States of America

ISBN: 978-1481946162

GrecoPress
~~P.O. Box 1752~~
~~Milton WA 98~~454

Chapters

Characters 1
Necropolis 10
Metropolis 14
Odyssey 17
Parliament 22
Cora 35
Pluto 50
Nomads 57
Pyrotechnics 63
Phosphoros 74
Necrology 87
Eros 98
Demos 103
Peripatetics 126
Callopolis 131
Cycles 143
Mythological Elements 161
About the Author 163

For Jeanie

Characters

Yellowpants Hellerman was watching, of course, from high in his watch-tower in The Great Dendron Tree, when he saw Cora and three of her favorite girl friends leave her house, wave goodbye to Cora's mother Demi and walk to a nearby field.

It was a strange corner of the field where they were going. It was rocky, so it was not useful for cultivation, though many had tried for eons to purge the earth of its stones. Despite this part of the field's being what untutored thinking considered useless, it had this attribute: for all its rockiness, it nourished a prolific array of wild flowers.

These sapling-waisted peach-breasted fifteen- and sixteen-year-old girls, so full of vitality, these semi-innocents, came to gather flowers to take to their mothers. What an abundance; what a variety of flowers there was in that patch – there were masses of carmine-colored peonies, spotted hyacinths, juniper-flavored amaryllis, glassy cosmos, cross-hatched rhododendrons, giant anemones, and myriads of green-headed irises.

The girls sat among the stones, chattering, picking flowers, and holding up floral treasures for one another to admire.

After a bit, Cora rose and wandered off, over a slight rise in the field to look for her favorite, a multi-headed narcissus. "Be right back," she said, leaving them gossiping. "Be right back," she repeated.

But she did not come back. All the girls would have had to do would have been to stand up and peer over the low rise before them, down to the road in the direction in which Cora had gone. They did not, naturally, so engaged were they in their chatter and gathering flowers. So they did not see what happened to her. However, from his perch in The Great Dendron Tree, Yellowpants Hellerman saw what happened.

After a few minutes, one of the girls asked casually, "What's become of Cora? Where is that girl?"

"Remember? She went after one of those narcissus," said another, not a bit bothered.

The girl who had raised the question at last stood, and peered down toward the road. She went to the top of the rise and looked around. As far as she could see in every direction, there was no sign of Cora. "I don't see her anywhere," she said, unconcerned. The other two stood and joined the first. They looked over at The Great Dendron Tree and called out, "Cora! Cora! Are you hiding from us? Come back now. Enough is enough."

One of the girls wandered over to the tree and walked around its vast base, increasing the pace of her steps and calling shrilly, "Cora! Cora!" The three took another look quickly and then scurried across the field and back to Cora's house to find Demi.

"Demi," they said, "Cora's missing. We don't know what's become of her. Maybe she's playing a game with us. Have you seen her, Demi? Is she here?" She was not.

Demi was startled. "What's this you are saying? What is this?" She asked the girls over and over again what had happened.

She strode to the field where they had been and she looked across the field from the top of the rising. She walked through the field, down toward the road. She half-ran to The Great Dendron Tree and looked around, but did not think to call out to Yellowpants Hellerman.

Word soon spread that Cora had disappeared. Various persons of notable authority and those of insatiable curiosity appeared at Demi's house asking about Cora. Demi, devastated as she was by the sudden disappearance of her beloved daughter, soon cleared everyone out. It was *her* work to find Cora. She paced about the house, frowning, talking to herself. She closed the door and bolted it, walking through the house. She picked up a walking stick and threw it aside. She closed the shutters to the windows.

Demi was indeed a woman of action. It was she who established the civilized world around her. She had brought the heathen, the wretched who had lived frayed and directionless lives, under her sway and taught them to settle down and plant and harvest, to build towns, to use streets instead of deer tracks, and to produce goods and open shops. It took Demi's time and energy to keep the experiment alive and growing. Now came this interruption, with her beloved daughter likely in danger.

"Think. Think," she told herself. "Think. Think. Think." Could this have been a random act? Could Cora have run away? Was she playing tricks? Was she hurt, or trapped or lost? Could she have been kidnapped? Demi ate nothing, and she became faint, but slept fitfully.

In the morning there came a knock on the door. It was Sophia, her older daughter, with her dog, night-black Cynique at her heels. "Yes?" said Demi, "Yes? Whatever is it? I'm busy."

"Ah," said Sophia, sensitive to the irritation in her mother's voice. "I'm sorry to bother you at this time," she said, "but then not entirely. You see, I have some useful information." Sophia was a person to whom information flowed as rivers to the sea, and she knew the power of knowledge. Trivia was the lifeblood of dark Sophia.

While Yellowpants Hellerman was far-seeing, in that he knew what he knew by what he observed and remembered (and what he observed and remembered extended far beyond the precincts of The Great Dendron Tree), Sophia was of a different order. She just knew things. She deduced things. She figured it out. She innately cast new light when new light was needed.

Sophia lived in a small house across the way from Demi and was on the road a good deal of the time, principally at night. She was a big woman, tall and well proportioned, but there was no avoiding the fact: she must be called *large*. Despite her imposing figure (who would dare tangle with her?), in the daylight she was pleasant to all and sundry, and she was liked by all and sundry. Folks round about who knew her gave her the pet name of "Moonbeam Sophia", in sweet derision.

They called this near-giant of a woman *Moonbeam* because of her enchantment with the moon. Gibbous? Waxing? Crescent? Waning? Always she was abroad in the light of the moon. She bathed in the light of the moon, storing up moonlight through lunar osmosis as one puts by food for the winter. In the night and the dark and the quiet, not only was she filled with the power of the moon, but knowledge flooded in upon her. She had her sources. She was a limitless receptacle of information. She did not question that which came her way. Nor was she overwhelmed by it. She absorbed it. She exulted in it, and when it was time to use what had entered her being, it flowed out as winds across the prairies.

She delightedly roamed the highways and byways, looking always for crossroads and searching out places where three roads came together, lighting her own way by means of a strange selenic aura which flowed from her softly, providing the light she needed on her way.

Always, on the dark nights or any-phase moon nights, Cynique, her night-black dog, was either at her heel or dashing miles ahead, returning with news. Sharp-sensed Cynique's nose and eyes to the ground brought back information about a fox with a damaged paw, about a hare that had been trapped, of furtive lovers who had just crossed a stile, and of oak and pine being burned for fuel in the gray hut with the moss-encrusted roof near the place where three roads crossed to the west.

Moonbeam Sophia looked into Cynique's massive black eyes and saw what Cynique saw, and knew what there was to know.

There was also an owl, Eulie by name, who accompanied Sophia. Eulie was a constant, coming and going overhead with news of the important and of the fragmentarily noteworthy.

Far-seeing Eulie flew from tree to tree, miles at a time, watching for mice and large moths, while serving Sophia by surveying the land from above. His eye-knowledge, taking in the broader details of life below, complemented Cynique's nose-knowledge. Eulie saw the order in which the stars were rising, which houses had no warming fires, which rivers were running high, and in which fields deer were feeding on the corn. When Sophia looked into Eulie's huge, glaucous eyes she saw what Eulie saw, and knew what there was to know.

"I was standing by the gate at the back of the house yesterday afternoon, across the street from you," said Sophia, "at the time that Cora disappeared, when I heard a sound that was strange. Maybe it was more than one sound, now that I think of it. I heard what I thought was a little cry, sort of a yelp, then the slamming of doors, and then I think the noise of horses and a carriage driving away, since shortly I couldn't hear any more."

"Tell me more!" demanded Demi.

"There is no more," responded Sophia, "I was behind the house, and I could not see the road, and I'm guessing about the carriage, but it's an accurate guess."

"A carriage. She was taken away in a carriage."

"Tell me," said Sophia, "Have you spoken to Yellowpants? I'm sure he saw the whole thing."

"No! Good Lord! Let's go. Is he in the tree?"

"Certainly. It's early." And they ran to The Great Dendron Tree.

"Yellowpants! Yellowpants!" they yelled as soon as they were in calling distance. "Can you hear us? Where are you?" But there was no response.

Yellowpants Hellerman was preoccupied. He had not been up in the tree long that morning and there was much to do. He had ridden his horse to the tree that morning as he did everyday. Yes, every single day, without fail, he rode his horse slowly from his house, nine miles to the west, stopping finally at The Great Dendron Tree on the lower corner of Miss Demi's farm. There he put his horse in a pasture and climbed the enormous tree where he spent the day near the top looking around him. Nothing escaped his view.

He saw everything there was to see in every direction, and nothing happened that he did not see. He stayed in the tree until it began to get dark, then he mounted his horse and letting it have its head, rode slowly home, circling around behind the farm and heading east by the upside road. At night he and his horse ate their fill, rested well, and were ready quite early the next day to ride back west toward the farm, where Miss Demi lived with her daughter, Cora, across the way from Sophia.

He observed huge flocks of geese skimming by on their migrations. He saw storms brooding in northern skies. He observed birds building their nests and raising their broods in the branches of the golden Dendron. He sheltered in the tree when gales whipped through. He watched shopkeepers in the village opening their doors for the day and shooing out wandering dogs, and he saw the child who was always late to school. But mostly he watched, keeping an eagle eye on those who passed up and down the road or worked in the fields or tended flocks. He didn't forget anything he saw. He remembered it all. He certainly saw what happened when Cora was snatched away, but he said nothing about it because no one had bothered to ask him what he knew.

Yellowpants Hellerman's mother did not think it strange that he left every morning on his horse for his place in the tree. She considered it his duty. "Someone has to keep a sharp eye on things," she said to herself more than once. "Someone needs to remember it all." Long, long ago she had bought a huge bolt of yellow canvas to make pants for her son. Periodically she would make him a new pair of pants when the old ones became threadbare with climbing around the rough bark of the ancient Dendron tree.

As pants they were not much for style. They were just a couple of round legs and seat and a waist without pockets. Just pants. Just functional pants. The marvel about the pants was the brightness of the color. Even when they were badly in need of replacement, they were still as bright, bright yellow as could be.

You could see him coming, even in the dark, a pair of yellow pants sitting on a horse, and you can see why he had long-since acquired his nickname, given him by the people he met as he rode his horse west or east. Even his mother, of all people, had forgotten his real name. She liked the nickname.

Everyone around those parts knew Yellowpants, and they all thought him odd. Who would spend all day every day, in a tree, never missing a day? Not even on holidays, not when the weather was severe, not even if the Acrobat of Heliopolis should happen to be performing next door, would he miss being in his tree, keeping an eye out for what was happening.

Those who knew him, or those who only passed him on the road and tipped their hats, thought him odd, but odd in the way that some children are thought odd because they can produce music on the lyre at age four, or at six can do sums in their heads at hyper speed. They are admired but certainly considered strange. Yellowpants had this reputation for knowing everything he had observed and not ever forgetting it, and when anyone happened to remember to ask Yellowpants about some event, some incident, he was sure to know. Yet because of what he did to accumulate this knowledge, they considered him strange, and, of course, kept their distance.

Demi and Sophia both shouted, "Yellowpants! Yellowpants. Can you hear us? It's very important that we speak with you."

A buzzing sort of voice answered. "I'm here, but I'm busy. What do you want of me?"

"Yellowpants, can you please come down and talk to us?"

"I cannot. I am occupied. A shepherd and his dog are moving some sheep to another pasture and the winds are shifting to the west which means a change in the weather, and there are some cowbirds plundering the maize, and my horse is going to the stream to get some water. I am very busy. Please let me get on with what I am doing."

"Yellowpants. I appreciate that you are very busy. Would you answer a question or two about something which happened yesterday, please, please, please?"

"Ask. But I do not like distractions! I can not abandon my work. The cowbirds are leaving. The sheep are almost in the other pasture and the dog is nipping the heels of the last sheep. The shepherd is lighting his pipe. He needs two matches in this wind."

"Yellowpants. Answer me this: did you see my daughter Cora yesterday?"

"Yes, I did."

"What did you see?"

"I saw her with three other girls picking flowers. I saw her stand up and go over the top of a little ridge. I saw her go down by the road. I saw her find a narcissus with many heads. I saw her pick it. The shepherd is having difficulty with his pipe. I saw a carriage stop. I saw two doors of the carriage open. I saw a man get out and walk over to her. I saw something in the man's hand.

"Oh, the shepherd has given up trying to light his pipe. The wind is dying down. I saw the man touch her with the thing in his hand. I saw her fall down. My horse is no longer at the stream. I saw the man pick her up. The little birds below me are trying to fly. I saw her swallowed up in the carriage. I saw it drive away. I saw the narcissus with many blooms lying on the ground. It is still there."

"Yellowpants," came a sobbing voice. "Yellowpants. Tell me about the carriage."

"It was big and long. Four doors on each side. Black. The windows were gold trimmed. There were four black horses."

Demi and Sophia looked at each other. "Who has such a carriage?" Demi asked.

"Tophat. Tophat DeVille," said Sophia immediately.

"Oh, my God. You're right," said Demi.

"DeVille," said Sophia.

"Yes. My dear brother. I absolutely hate him. He of The Necropolis," she said.

"I know," said Sophia.

"I went to The Necropolis once," said Demi. "The minute I arrived at The Necropolis DeVille appeared and said I could only stay a moment. I visited my mother's grave; then I left."

Necropolis

Tophat DeVille was the owner of the world famous Necropolis. Every day there were hundreds, if not thousands, of funerals there. The processions of the living and the dead would have made this city of the dead intolerably congested if it had not been so large. Indeed it had many levels below the earth. Tophat and his cohorts had found a way to construct burial sites beneath the earth in a manner which defied all conventional engineering understanding of the possible.

Below ground it was dreary and cold. A few pitiful lights haphazardly guided processions to burial sites in the Stygian blackness. Dreary creeks of dripping water infested the passages. In these Dantesque levels, the graves were poor chock-a-block shallowish pits, with little accommodation for visitors who might wish to visit their dead after the funerals

However, this cemetery was immense. Those proceeding into the stifling darkness of the lower depths could not have helped noticing there was a different sort of burial place on the surface level — for those whose survivors were willing to pay fees that would make extortionists seem like agents of grace. In the fresh air, this resting place was a thing of beauty. Hectares of narcissus and jonquils, kilometers of asphodels and daffodils abounded perpetually, all beloved of Tophat DeVille.

Streams ran through the grounds, their banks edged with minty chervil bushes and tarragon trees. Bridges wide enough for grand processions crossed over the streams, and wide, smoothly paved roads led from one section of the grounds to another.

Mourners in these happier grounds wore more cheerful faces. The elite suffered less seeing the marvels of the carved stones. (The rules of The Necropolis permitted only up-lifting carvings, such as baby angels whose wings were widespread in impish poses.)

Mausoleums fit for Persian satraps were scattered about, but open, airy in aspect, welcoming to the dear recently departed as well as mourners who bore picnic luncheons. Brightly-hued columbaria and tartanned ossuaries abounded. Indeed many visitors to this wondrous place did bring food and drink and enjoyed themselves as do Peruvians in camposantos on All Saints Day.

Yet after experiencing the gorgeous grounds, the feelings of visitors who searched for those who rested below, and who were depressed by the gloom of the lower depths, were salved, knowing that this beautiful place above ground existed, and they only wished that the very knowledge of the existence of this paragon of elegance might provide comfort to their dear recently departed, damply ensconced for eternity below.

It was to The Necropolis that Demi and Sophia determined Cora had been forcibly taken. "Why, and for what purpose, was she taken there?" they asked. To Demi it was clear she could not go and demand her daughter's return. She would be immediately ejected.

Here Sophia provided comfort, even to Demi, who one would not have thought of as being open to suggestions, who could not possibly have conceived of herself as needing help. But Demi deferred to Sophia from time to time. Sophia, do not forget, was even more knowledgeable about what was going on in the world than Yellowpants Hellerman. Sophia was a woman of resources.

Sophia had been thinking about Cora's kidnapping by Tophat. "I believe," she said, "that he acted out of spite to show that he could do it, and from his unbending desire to have such a beauty by his side. I know, and you know, that Cora is unhappy and how she wants to be freed from his grasp. But, but," she warned. "It's an old, old story that sometimes the captives become entranced with those who hold them captive. We must set her free quickly."

"So, let's see what *we* can do," Sophia said, making the daring assumption that Demi would allow such a thing. Demi stared at her daughter for a long time, thinking about what Sophia had said, and then decided to let her into her life, if only in a guarded manner.

"All right. What shall *we* do?"

Sophia, glad that Demi would consider her help, said "We must seek help from the highest sources; we must find Uncle Theo. It won't be easy, but we must find him. We'll have to look for people who know where he is. Theo is our only hope. Let's find him. Let's leave right now. We can rescue Cora."

"This won't be good," said Demi. "This may take time and I've never been away from this place for more than a day or two, not long enough for anyone to realize that I've gone. I know there'll be consequences if I'm gone for some time."

"I understand what you're saying," said Sophia, the seer, the prophetess. "You're afraid that in your absence everything will stop. People will not know what to do. They're so used to your presence. You're their guiding light. You make sense of life for others."

"That is true," answered Demi. "Not that it's always a good thing, is it? I've often asked myself.

"But," she said, "There's nothing else to do but bring Cora back safely. How long do you think we will be gone?"

Sophia looked deep within herself and then said, "About ten days. We'll accomplish our goal in ten days."

It was true that Demi had seldom left her property. She was the one who had conceived of the possibilities here for the production of food. She was the one who organized the people. She had been out and among them and trained them in working the land, and she had made them a productive society. She took great pride in her work. Now there were villages on her property. Now there were flourishing shops and tradesmen in the villages. Now there was commerce from afar. And yet, there was something about Demi which was necessary, of the essence of these vast holdings of hers. She was so integrated in the work, in the life of this great place that she had become as necessary as water, or earth, or air, or fire.

"All right," said Demi. "Let's get on our way."

So, off they went. Yellowpants Hellerman saw them hurry over the rise where Cora had crossed, down the field, and onto the lane where the carriage had taken Cora in front of Demi's place. He saw them turn to the right and watched them until they were out of sight.

Metropolis

By mid-afternoon, after Demi and Sophia had disappeared from view, a dark grayish mist began to cover all of Demi's immense holdings. It did not appear as fog rolling in from the sea, but rather it arose from the earth itself, as steam begins to rise from a pan of water over fire. It increased in intensity and soon strained visibility. From the top of his tree Yellowpants Hellerman puzzled at this gray matter, which clouded his view from the ground up. Seeing that it was not going to dissipate and that the sun was no longer visible, he climbed down. Without any urging his faithful horse trotted over to him, ready to make the journey to the comfort of his stall. He carried Yellowpants homeward with some urgency.

The next morning the dark mist prevailed till nearly mid-morning. The cocks did not crow to wake the world, though they often crowed while it was still dark. This morning they were unaccustomedly silent, for they could not sense the arrival of day. Yellowpants did not arrive at The Great Dendron Tree until well after ten o'clock.

Yellowpants saw people from the vassal villages coming to the farm looking for their milk, for the milkmaids had failed to appear on time and the cows were in the fields moaning for lack of milking. Yellowpants saw the villagers butt their heads against the cows' sides and place buckets under the cows and begin for themselves the laborious challenge of milking. He saw tradesmen and servants and workers looking about for what to do, directionless, disoriented. Demi was gone and no one was in charge.

That day, the day after Demi and Sophia had left, the dark mist appeared even earlier in the afternoon, so that Yellowpants, who had not had a particularly busy day, called it quits around three p.m. He mounted his nervous steed and up around the top of Demi's vast holdings they went, heading east for food and rest, arriving in the dark at an oddly early hour.

So it went, with the dark mist covering the land and sky later and later each day, and settling in again ever earlier. After some days, the mist was there to stay. Yellowpants abandoned his ritual trip to the Dendron tree. He stayed in bed. He sat by the fire. He read a book, but could not concentrate. He felt out of sorts, dislocated, beside himself. Uselessly he looked out of the windows, hoping for clearing skies.

It was quiet everywhere. The birds huddled on branches they could barely see, fearful of leaving their haven. Cows remained in the fields, grazing automatically, though their hearts were not in it. They were unmilked so they became dry. No one saw to them.

The predators, the raptors for whom in the face of such lethargy this would have been a lovely time, stayed in their lairs, their appetites gone, their interest in the hunt, their penchant for group hunting immobilized.

Gloom settled on the people of the region. In the midst of hopelessness, of general apathy, families lost their sense of unity. The energy normally evoked by ad hoc committees, liturgical gatherings, thesis committees, training groups, court hearings, and caucuses was passionless.

Nor did any take pleasure in the warmth of the human touch. Holding an infant close to one's cheek meant nothing. Shy first-time hand-holding had no appeal. Quiet cuddling with a loved one gave no gentle delight. The sight of a long-absent loved one coming through the door awakened scant interest. Cats no longer followed old men about the house.

When there was conversation among these lost people, it was about how awful the situation was. How could it be? How long might it go on? Most concluded that the unfortunate life-smothering weather was connected to the absence of Demi. Until she returned, they estimated, there would be no change in the order of things. It would be perpetual night, and nothing could grow; nothing could proceed.

It was all too hopeless. But, some did dare to hope. One couple dared to think that something might be made of the dark mist, that there could be new, creative ways of looking at the situation in which they found themselves. Something, they believed, could be done if there were the will. But – but – they were summarily waved off as troublemakers by wiser heads who knew that the cause was lost until Demi returned. Some of these gathered every day to think about Demi and to dream about what life had been like when she was on the job, yes, even when she was simply present. Though they were not normally given to prayer, they prayed for the restoration of the olden days.

Odyssey

Demi and Sophia started off and Yellowpants saw them turn the corner and then they were lost from view. Around the corner, Demi and Sophia walked swiftly to the west, Cynique trotting just ahead of them. They endlessly discussed their situation, repeating what they knew again and again, as if by doing so, their discussion would open a crack in the earth into which they would fall, which would then lead them to Uncle Theo.

As they strode along, it occurred to Sophia to ask Demi, "Why are we walking? Wouldn't we find Uncle Theo faster if we went in your coach?"

Demi replied, "But that's not the way to find Theo. We would speed along at such a pace that we would miss the signs he leaves pointing the way to him."

"Of course," said Sophia, "Of course. How could I forget? He leaves signs along the way. We're walking in the direction that DeVille's coach went, which is the way we should begin. All of Uncle Theo's signs will point the way we should go. If we started in any other direction it would be a waste of time."

"Precisely. You are so clever," said Demi. "To find Theo we must be in tune with the nature of our surroundings and look for the unexpected. Say, don't you feel the way the ground moves our feet? Don't you feel it tugging us in this direction?"

"Yes. I feel it. It's strong. It *is* strong."

Uncle Theo loved leaving clues, for there was much of the comedian about him. Theo delighted in enabling people to find him when they needed him, though he was not a believer in making it easy. Why should it be easy to find one of such importance as he? It should take work. It should be transformative, even for such distinguished persons as Sophia and Demi.

All of his hints, clues, signs, omens – whatever – were based in nature, but were in their context unnatural, physically unexpected. If you were alert, you might, for example, detect the smell of new sawdust when there were no sawmills near, or clean alpine air when you were in lowlands. Then, if you did, you could be assured you were on track.

When you crossed a creek, the music of the water could be singing a nursery tune if you paid any attention. In another coursing of water, there might be peculiar icy green bubbles skittering along. And if you happened to see these extraordinary bubbles, you could be assured you were on the right path.

Oh yes, sometimes there could be tiny red flowers leaning in one direction when the breeze was blowing in another. And, if you were to pick a petal from one of the leaves and chew on it, it would taste acrid at first, but then it would melt into such sweetness that you would claw at these flowers and stuff them in your mouth to relive that experience – another sign that you were on track.

There would be other signals of Theo's having passed that way: a slight shivering of leaves on an amaryllis bush, an unexpected grove of celosia trees; fearless, speckled bucks blocking the way, and the scent of cinnamon wafting from no discernable place.

The sky was also a source, but easily overlooked, it being too obvious. Even the wisest, the most sophisticated, could overlook the brazen cloudforms and skycolors holding messages for them, practically clamoring at them, begging them to gaze up and read the messages in the heavens.

If the clues took careful observation, it should be noted they were ephemeral. Were Demi and Sophia to look back, to retrace their steps to be sure of what they had seen, they would have been disappointed. Gone. The clues would have disappeared as surely as yesterday.

As they continued their march, they were accompanied by the persistent tattoo of faraway tympani. The sound enveloped them. Its beat stirred them. The distant sound joined the earth underfoot and moved with them.

As they walked purposely onward, all life around them became aware of the sound. In the thrall of the thrumming, every plant stood unaccustomedly tall. Deer and all other animals' heads swiftly raised in reaction, as if to danger, bodies tense, poised to flee, until the drumming and Demi and Sophia passed on and the silence of the natural world returned. Then the plants relaxed and the animals returned to their work of grazing.

That night the two sheltered under a cedar tree. They picked great handfuls of clematis blossoms to lay their heads on. They gathered armfuls of soft anthurium to make their beds. Then, draping their cloaks about them, they quickly fell asleep.

Sophia slept an hour before she wakened to walk along the road for her moonbath, Cynique bounding on ahead, gathering information in a strange land. When Moonbeam Sophia returned to the Cedar tree she slept the sleep of the confident, as Demi slept the sleep of the fitful. The owl, Eulie, hooted his news above them.

In the morning they followed a path where they had seen a bi-crested black sparrow. Before long they came upon a trading post at a place where three ways met. As they neared the building, the drumming about them increased its intensity. Standing tall and majestic, they entered the post, and those within fell back, cowering at their presence. The drumming sound fell upon them as a heavy rain upon a roof. Demi and Sophia approached the keeper to ask if he had seen Uncle Theo of late.

The keeper was standing as far back from the counter as he could, hiding behind his large apron, trying to make himself as insignificant as he could. He answered in a low, faltering voice, "He passes by here on his way to other places and I dare not ask him anything. Sometimes he pays for what he needs and sometimes he doesn't, and I fear asking him." Then the keeper said, "I have been expecting you. You are Demi, I believe," bowing ever so slightly.

"I am indeed. How is it that you have been expecting me?"

"Ah, yes. Well. Theo left a package for you. He said you would know what to do with it." He handed her a heavy round package. Demi took the package and the two, out of caution, went out into the sunshine to open it. They removed four separate layers of silken paper before they found its contents: a beautiful apple-sized golden ball. It was not a ball of blinding brightness, but coldly dull gold. Amazed, Sophia and Demi inspected this heavy treasure. In a moment they found an engraving in small clear letters, which said simply, "Theo". There was more on the other side, plainly written in larger letters, "For the fairest".

"So, it is Theo's," said Demi, "and it is 'For the fairest'. What can that mean?"

Sophia said, "It clearly means 'For the most beautiful', but…" she said, engaging the wheels of her intellectual powers, "…clearly, 'fairest' can mean more than one thing. Let me see; it seems that Uncle Theo has left us with a puzzle. He's playing a little game with us once again. He knows we want to find him and he's leading us on. We appear to be going in the right direction. Let's continue."

"I agree," said Demi, unaccustomed as she was to admitting the wisdom of others.

They bought a bit of food in the trading post. Outside, they looked about for the way to go, for there were three choices. One of the paths led upward; and they could see along that way a small cairn of blue hematite. "That is the way," said Sophia. They had just passed the cairn when Sophia turned back to collect one of the odd stones, but it was no more.

They marched on that day as if through a desert, as if across high mountains and along the sea. They slept that night under folds of a twisted archimedean tree, wrapped in their cloaks, upon bushels of yellow dianthan blossoms. Moonbeam Sophia walked to absorb the light of the moon. Cynique was at her heel, and Eulie the owl followed noiselessly from tree to tree.

Parliament

The next morning they wakened hungry and continued their march. Four wild hares busied themselves building a nest on the path, unconcerned with the passers-by. They were now in unfamiliar territory, but were certain of their direction. Sophia said, "We're about to come across a very large gathering of people. I learned that last night." In an hour they mounted a stretch of low hills and beheld below a monumental basilica and thousands and thousands of busy people dressed in black, coming and going, to and from the building. Many smaller buildings surrounded the massive structure.

As Demi and Sophia neared the site of all this activity they saw a sign reading "Biennial Parliament of Judges. Welcome to the Hall of Justice". "Now we know," said Demi, sagely, "why they are all wearing black robes."

Where is Theo leading us now? Why are we here? Demi asked herself. The basilica before them was a vast building, its roof resting on massive columns. A large and welcoming narthex opened onto the building. Signs on each of the columns indicated for the unilluminated which columns had Doric capitals, which Ionic and which Corinthian. The interior of the building was so designed that it focused on an apse at the opposite end from where Demi and Sophia and Cynique entered. There on a raised platform was a massive chrysolite table onto which many examples of tansy plants had been exquisitely incised.

Comfortable chairs such as one finds in exclusive clubs filled the hall, and black-robed men sat chatting in small groups. Many stared at nothing, doubtless contemplating matters judicial, while hoping it would not be long until sherry hour. Others milled about waiting for sessions to begin. Still others nodded off from the arduous business of a convention of judges. More were dining in the various cafes and restaurants.

As they walked into the building, Demi and Sophia drew within themselves. They became shorter, inconspicuous. Their cloaks nearly covered them. Once inside the massive structure, Sophia drew Demi's attention to the plethora of signs lining the walls of the building. They walked over to inspect them and found an hourly schedule of the convention's lectures and seminars. A separate schedule called attention to practice sessions for mock trials and moot courts, held six times a day.

Notice was also given that at noon each day there were actual trials of miscreants of various orders. This notice assured the honorable judges that justice would be swift in these cases simply because the convention's schedule did not allow for over-much judicial contemplation.

Another series of signs, larger in print than the others, took pleasure in notifying the conventioneers that (for their convenience) the restaurants and pubs had no closing hours. Other signs pointed to The Village where purveyors of goods needed by the honorable judges could conveniently be found.

As Demi and Sophia wandered through the basilica, they saw a countless number of kiosks which provided services and information. "We must be in The Village," said Demi. "Let's see what this is about." They found that in the "Village", in accordance with tradition, kiosks of the same type were grouped together, as rows of shoe shops were once in the agoras of ancient cities.

They came upon two kiosks where black caps were for sale. Judges, of course, were in the habit of placing such caps on their heads at the time of pronouncing extremely bad news for the prisoner in the dock. It was enlightening to see how many varieties of caps there were, not to mention the quality of the material from which the caps were made. It was equally apparent from the flurry of business that the frequent use of the caps meant that replacement was often necessary, just as it is required to replace collars and cuffs on shirts which become frayed with over-use. The two kiosks carried different stock, appealing to distinct bodies of clients, though it is just possible that the competition between them was more apparent than real, since there was some evidence that both were owned by the same entrepreneur.

Demi said, "There is something strange here. Things don't ring true." Her observation started Sophia thinking.

When they found shops selling "Scales of Justice," they found, remarkably, every possible form of "Scales of Justice" was for sale. Full-sized scales, actual scales from all over the world, as well as decorative ones for wearing. Copies of famous works of art featuring Lady Justice were offered, as well as swords of various types and sizes. The travelers, having taken in the wondrous display of scales, walked on. Demi said grimly, "I am truly beginning to have an unpleasant feeling about all this."

"I know what you're talking about," said Sophia.

Just then they passed a booth, which caught their attention with a sign that proclaimed "Little Latin?" A professorial spokesman was admonishing a group of rapt judges that Latin was no less important now than it ever had been in the legal profession. "But," the classics scholar continued, "…we in the Latin trade have noticed that there is a slackening of interest in the language, although as you know full well, it is still essential in everyday use at the office.

"You may have used your Latin when you studied law at your university. Alternatively, you may have read for the bar while working in an office. If so, you well remember that, as apprentices, you read documents in Latin, when you were not running to the courts with forgotten documents or fetching pots of tea for the lawyers, barristers, attorneys, counselors, and solicitors who inhabited the office."

The salesman was enticing the passers-by to buy his company's Latin textbooks.

"Let's move along. I don't like this one bit," said Demi and marched off with Sophia while Cynique led the way.

The two realized that they had been so taken with the booths and kiosks that they had not stopped to have anything to eat. Aware there was no end of possibilities of food they entered the Dining Hall, and chose a relatively clean table, and breakfasted well.

As they ate, Demi saw across the hall a sign reading "All Sorts of Courts". After paying the bill, they walked across to this spot where they saw two lists of courts.

List A noted Civil Courts, Circuit Courts, Small Claims Courts, Supreme Courts, Traffic Courts, Criminal and Civil Courts, Tax Courts, Appeals Courts, and Circuit Courts.

List B included Drumhead Courts, Kangaroo Courts, Show Trial Courts, Star Chamber Courts, Summary Justice Courts, Lynch Mob Courts, Posse Comitatus Courts, and Closed Door Courts.

Sophia asked the proprietors of the booth what they were about, since there were no apparent explanations.

"Ah, yes, I don't wonder that you should ask. We have a lot of people asking why we are here and we are considering the possibility of placing a sign alongside the others, which explains our *raison d'être*. That's French, you know."

"Thank you for that information," said Sophia, "do go on."

"The reason we are here is to help our clientele understand the role of each of these courts. Therefore we sponsor court cases, real cases, in which we have judges from various courts presiding in courts they are unaccustomed to. For example, just today we had a panel of actual Supreme Court justices presiding in a traffic court dealing with the case of a man who stole an apple from a vendor. Earlier in the day, a justice of the peace official heard a case of discrimination against women in the work place, or was that the one in which there was a lake front boundary dispute between two states? I am sorry to be confused. We offer so many opportunities for our judges to widen their perspectives."

"What about list 'B?" asked Demi, "You know, show trials and the like."

"Well, we try to keep an open mind here," said the proprietor. "These trials – show trials, kangaroo trials and the like – evolved for a reason through the ages, and we try to keep an historic perspective on them. We try to demonstrate that they have their uses and advantages, even though they have been much disparaged in the liberal, single-minded, biased press.

"So," he continued, "as a help to the judiciary, we do hold trials of these sorts, which are, *por supuesto* (he said, generously displaying his multi-linguistic abilities,) of course, real trials. These are no mock trials that make a mockery of the system. Here a Star Chamber Trial is a real Star Chamber trial and Summary Justice is meted out. What ever would be the worth of holding 'pretend' trials? This way the judges, the lawyers for the defense, and the prosecuting lawyers have something they can seriously get their teeth into.

"Accordingly, on the other side of this building," he said gesturing to his left, "you will find the justice-meting room. There you will find simple stocks in which convicted persons are placed with ample room for taunting activities and an extensive list of aspersions to be cast, and cells for solitary confinement, and seamstresses ready to sew the letter "A" or other letters on shirts or dresses, as appropriate. You understand, I know. The whole gamut is covered by the Parliament to provide for the needs of the convicted. What good would it be if it were all 'pretend', I ask you? This is serious business we are in here."

"Does that include…?" asked Sophia, with some hesitation.

"I think you are referring to, shall we say, 'final disposition'. Indeed, various methods are provided in the same justice-meting room, according to law and according to how the judge happens to feel on the day he reaches into his robe for his black cap."

"Thank you for this instructive time," said she. "My dear and honorable mother, don't you think it is time we moved on?" Sophia whispered, "I am feeling disgusted, but let us not forget that we have work to do here."

"Work? What sort of work do we have to do here?" asked Demi. Sophia opened the parcel she had been carrying.

The golden ball peeked out. "Oh, my goodness, I had forgotten the ball."

"Remember what is written on the ball?"

"Yes, I do," said Demi. "'Theo,' and 'For the Fairest'. Now I see why Theo has led us here."

"What do you mean?" asked Sophia.

"You will see," came the answer.

As they walked, Demi said to Sophia, "I agree. This is a disgusting place… with disgusting people."

"Indeed they are," replied Sophia. "They are like fancy liturgists who surround themselves with presbyters and acolytes and deacons – the full panoply – who go through their liturgies completely ignoring what they are truly about, so absorbed by their colorful vestments and swinging smoky pots and clanging bells."

"Yes," said Demi, "These people are pseudo-, pseudo-what?"

"'Pseudo-sophists?" suggested Sophia.

"Yes. That is good. Yet, if they are pseudo are they truly sophists?"

The two continued their walk through The Village toward their next adventure. Along the way they passed a Robery, where hundreds of judicial robes were on offer. The display was almost exclusively of traditional black robes. However, in the back of the shop one might find a few garments on which the cut of the sleeves had been daringly altered, noticeable only by the most astute eye, and a few robes with a subtle suggestion of color along the shoulder line. A small but prominently displayed sign announced that the tailors were on hand to cut robes from the finest of materials for the discriminating judges, with delivery guaranteed within 48 hours.

Their anger rising, the two quickly passed by a shop entitled "Hammermacher", purveyor of gavels and their accessories. Another shop featured a large assortment of chairs for the use of judicial bottoms while their owners were presiding at court. Yet another sold books with erudite titles which were incomprehensible but which provided an aura of *je ne sais quoi* to fill the oak shelving in the judges' un-read libraries. Finally, before they tired of window shopping, they saw a kiosk which sold lamps such as Diogenes was purported to have used in his search for an honest man.

They walked away from The Village grousing about the falseness of it all and found themselves in the narthex of the Basilica. Looking at the stage, Sophia said, "The judges are beginning to assemble. Look at those pompous… what are they called?… oh yes, hierarchs. Look at how those *hierarchs* are seating themselves daintily upon their thrones. Wouldn't this be a fine time to raise the question here in this assembly about who among them is the fairest?"

"Yes," said Demi, "Let's walk up there and have at them." So, they began to walk down the main aisle: Demi and Sophia, with Cynique walking regally ahead of them. Eulie, Sophia's owl, took advantage of the moment, with the judges bustling to find places, the very time when all eyes were also focused on the stage, to fly unnoticed into the basilica and land on a towering Corinthian capital with its inviting perch-holds.

The main reason Eulie hid was he did not want to cause disruption. He knew that he, the symbol of wisdom, was anathema to judges who suffered what Eulie called "sophia-phobia". Who among them would want their courtly decisions scrutinized by wisdom, any more than unbound passion seeks the commanding voice of reason?

Many of the judges had spent an inordinate amount of time in Athens studying the laws of old, and had become paranoid about the incessant presence of the city's owls, which peered over their shoulders and made derisive noises. "Strigiphobes!" Eulie jeered at them. "Glaucophobes! Owl-fearers," he hooted to himself. Eulie wisely kept himself out of sight.

As noted earlier, when Demi and Sophia had been meandering through the building, they had gathered themselves in, were mousey in affect, small in stature, drawing little notice, not even a normal masculine second glance.

Now, as they processed along the long aisle toward the platform in the apse, they pulled themselves erect, straightened themselves up, as if regenerating themselves, and became tall, very tall, and colorful… commanding. They moved along the aisle as if they were on the bow of a great-prowed bireme on the wine dark sea, dividing the waters deeply. The thrumming, drumming which followed the two on their mission intensified. The black-robed ones gathering in the rows of seats, shifted to left or to right away from the aisle, pressing up against one another as if to avoid a tsunami. A low groaning of fear arose among them, which amused Demi and Sophia, who seemed to grow taller and taller as they processed regally toward the apse, now seven feet tall, now ten, it seemed.

Ahead of them the hierarchy was seated on the Platform of Power. Over the central throne was the title "The Paragon". To his left, seated a little lower, was "The Parabolist". On the right, also at a lower level, was "The Paradigmist".

Even these eminences, accustomed to all manner of people, from serfs to sires, presenting themselves before the court, were noticeably fearful of the mysterious approaching beings. The hierarchs shrank back against their thrones, as if willing themselves to be threaded through whatever cracks in the wood their bodies could find. They yowled and yipped. Their faces were distorted, as if great blasts of wind were funneled against them.

At last Demi and Sophia, led by Cynique, reached the stage. With no hesitation they mounted the stairs, heedless of protocol, careless of etiquette. The intensity of the drumbeats continued, now muted.

The two were amused as they stood before the cowering Judge of Judges and said in one voice, "Honorable and Reverend Sir, we come on a mission."

After a prolonged silence, the Paragon gathered himself together and, in an abnormal, high-pitched voice, said "Pray tell, what is your mission?"

"It is this," said Demi, placing the golden ball before them. "We have this gift for you. It is for the one among you in this vast gathering who is the fairest."

Trembling, the Paragon of judges took the ball and, studying it, asked, "And, pray, what, noble persons, do you believe is meant by *fairest*?"

Sophia spoke, a detectable sneer in her voice, saying, "I would have thought it would be obvious, honorable sir. Do you mean to say that you do not know which judge among you is the fairest in his judgments?"

The Paragon of Paragons shivered and shook, not knowing what to say, for he was fearful of saying the wrong thing. He was fearful of angering these powerful ones who stood before him. In fear he said, "Pray tell us what it is that you mean."

There was momentary silence in the hall. Each black robe was frozen and attentive as never before in their lives, for they had no idea what the consequences of the encounter with these magnificent creatures could be. But soon the clamor began anew as each searched others for the meaning of the intrusion.

Sophia said to the Paragon, "To be plain, it simply means, who in this gathering of thousands and thousands of judges, judges the most fairly. Who among you is the fairest judge of all? Do you understand now?" she said, stressing every word.

This conversation had taken place in a loud tone, but because of the increasing din in the astounded assembly, it could only been heard by Demi and Sophia, and by the exalted ones and their sycophants sitting on the platform. The Paragon responded, "I beg your pardon, O Mighty Ones, but how does anyone know who is the most fair at trials? I myself have a good reputation or I would presume that I would not be seated where I am."

"Let us see about that," said Demi. She turned and faced the assemblage of black gowns and said demosthenically, "Who among you is the fairest?"

The crowd, which had been overwhelmed by the appearance of the illustrious two, was standing, bobbing and weaving about, and pointing at the two, anxiously yelling back and forth to one another in hopes of discovering someone who might know who the two were. Such was the uproar; such was their fear. Demi was forced to repeat her question. She was forced to repeat it several more times before the black robes calmed down and not only began to pay attention to the question but actually understood it. "Who is the fairest? Tell me now."

There was silence for a few minutes as the judges seemed to be meditating on this sacred question. Then came low whispers and the nodding of heads in the assembly. Then the hubbub of low conversations began. The level of their discussion soon began to rise as it became apparent that not only had they understood the question, but that there were differences of opinion, particularly since every person in the vast arena began to proclaim themselves clearly the fairest.

Then came the clamoring. Uproar! Confusion! The judges rose from their seats to express their opinions about themselves and to criticize their colleagues' assertions, who in turn were scandalized that their opinions of themselves were received so caustically. Now two rose together and, standing precariously on their seats, debated their differences of opinion with sarcastic jabs, punches, and kicks. Some left their seats to confront fellow judges across aisles who were making satirical remarks about them and their assertions they were perfectly fair in all judgments. Oh, the diatribes! Oh, the philippics! Oh, the anathemas!

The Paragon pounded with his gavel, shouting "Order, order, order!" but availed nothing against the cacophony. Finally he turned to Demi and Sophia and said, "This is your fault. If you want an answer, you call them to order."

"*Avec plaisir*," Demi said, showing off for the judge. She turned to the black-robed mob. Pointing a long, bejeweled finger at them she said, "Be still! Be still!" elongating the words elegantly. "Let there be S-I-L-E-N-C-E!"

All began to quiet down. The mobsters began to return to their seats, still grumbling and grousing. After a while it was mostly quiet in the hall, though there was still an undercurrent of noise as whispered attacks on one another continued.

Demi approached the rim of the stage. "Be silent," she ordered. "Not one word," she said, and there was silence, except for the beat of the drums. She walked slowly down the steps and began walking along the aisle, her eyes filled with thunder. As she walked, she looked deeply into the eyes of the black-robed mob. Many looked away.

"You are a catastrophe," she said. "From the moment we entered this building it has been clear that you are false. All you are interested in are the trappings of your office. You care more about holding office and playing at being judges than you do at meting out justice fairly. You curry favor. You dismiss views other than your own. No wonder the Gods are contemptuous." Holding aloft the golden ball for all to see, she added, "We came here seeking the fairest of you all, but it is clear that there is no one here worthy of this prize. Indeed the word 'pseudo' has been invented just for you. You are false. You are liars!"

As she walked along the aisle, towering over them, the judges again fell back into one another to avoid her. "What has happened to you? Where is there a Nestor among you? Where is Solon? Where is there a Mentor? Gone. Rooted out by the enforcement of shallowness, by self-service. Where is there humility? You are a catastrophe."

She turned back to look at the stage and beckoned to Sophia and to Cynique. "Come Sophia. Come here, Cynique. There is no one worthy here. Here," she pronounced, "there is no one fair."

As they walked regally out of the building the drumming became deafening. Eulie swooped down from his perch and flew over the crowd several times. He swirled, he dove, he spun, he circled, he sailed. He enjoyed himself. The judges quickly spied the owl and pointed him out to one another. A sharp keening arose among them as they saw the dreaded symbol of wisdom. Paroxysms of fear arose among the black robes. They believed themselves cursed. Tumbling over one another they began to scatter for the exits. In one last energetic diving act Eulie flew out the open door and disappeared from view, but not before discharging upon the judges a widespread caca-bomb.

Demi, Sophia, Cynique, and Eulie gathered on the broad path outside of the parliament. "What next?" asked Sophia. "That effort failed. We still have the golden ball to give to the fairest. Do we continue? Where do we go?

"We have to find Uncle Theo. We must find Cora. That Tophat has her!" She added, "We must find someone who fits the description of 'the fairest.' We must go on. But which way do we go?"

Demi gazed all about her. To her left she saw a path that led through a low bower of golden eucalyptus trees. "This is the way. That's the sign," she said. They marched to the bower and through it. When Sophia looked back some minutes later, the trees were gone.

CORA

When DeVille drugged Cora, she fell heavily. DeVille caught her, scooped her into his arms, and swiftly placed her into the back seat of the coach, hoping no one had seen him. As he climbed into the coach he reached back and snapped off a multi-headed narcissus, ignoring the one Cora had dropped. He sat beside her and pulled her inert body against him, keeping his arm around her to keep her from slumping over. Her long black hair fell against his face and he delighted in its faint cinnamon scent and in the closeness of her body.

He placed his narcissus on the seat beside her and rapped his cane against the ceiling of the coach. He said in a semi-whisper, "Not too fast. Mind the bumps."

The journey to The Necropolis was long – longer than normal because DeVille had no intention of waking Cora. Besides, he was enjoying this time with her, unconscious though she was. He had coveted her from the time that she had begun to blossom into young womanhood. He could not help patting her helenic face and moving his hands gently across the softness of her unconscious body.

Through the night and into the next day they traveled at a leisurely pace. By noon they reached the main road to The Necropolis. They had not gone far on this road before it became massively congested with the crowds of people traveling to the cemetery with their late-beloveds in tow.

There were hearses and stretchers bearing the dead. Carts and tumbrels and shopworn catafalques. Squadrons carried inert forms aloft, and military parades marched to muffled drums. Some beloved were borne in wheelbarrows; some were draped over horses; other bodies displayed signs their lives had been recently and publicly ended. Certain of those on the road carting mortal remnants pushed and shoved their way through the crowds, clearly in a hurry, delighted to lay their charges to rest, they hoped, in perpetual oblivion.

The driver of Tophat's carriage soon turned off the impassable road to an unlikely looking lane, which led at length to a private entrance into The Necropolis. There the carriage made its way through the inviting Elysian grounds where happy mourners picnicked among the crowds of daffodils. On rolled the coach around a corner. It passed the entrance to the underground burials, that doleful, muddy place where the hoi polloi carried their dead for want of position or funds to bury them above.

They pulled up at DeVille's mansion, and a servant, Melantha, happened to meet the coach. DeVille ordered her to scurry off and to prepare the finest room in the mansion for Cora. DeVille lifted Cora – Cora of the slight body, of the dark, dark hair and eyebrows, Cora of the faintly bronzed skin, Cora the peach-breasted, Cora the long coveted, out of the carriage. He carefully carried her down long corridors, one after another, until he arrived at the room chosen and prepared by Melantha. There he gently placed her on a pillowed sofa. DeVille stood admiring her, before he himself tenderly covered her with a silken sheet and kissed her forehead.

Melantha observed DeVille and Cora closely. DeVille looked up and considered her. "Melantha," he said, "from now on you are to be her guardian and her companion. You must be with her and available to her at all times. She'll be frightened and anxious when she wakes up, for she'll be disoriented. But you'll be able to help her. You'll offer her sympathy. You will console her. You will gradually introduce her to The Necropolis.

"She is to be my bride, Melantha, but I'm not in a hurry because I have other satisfactions. I'll slowly and gradually introduce myself to her. She'll not see me at first, or even know about me. Then I'll begin to appear, but only in the distant background. When she first sees me, it will mean nothing, I'll be just another person in the background. Only gradually will I become a presence to her.

"So, I entrust her well-being to you. Please do not permit her to leave this room for a while. Provide for her every need. And then the day will come when you'll take her for a walk in the sunshine. You will prepare her for The Necropolis.

"Oh, and Melantha, please change your clothing. You're so darkly dressed. You'll scare her by your very appearance."

"But Sir," said Melantha, "I like my clothes. They fit me. They fit my personality."

"That may be," said DeVille, "but surely you can do something. Add a little color here and there – a bit of ribbon, perhaps, or a colorful sash around your waist. Surely you can do something. I fear you'll frighten this child with your austerity. You could stand a bit of washing up, too."

"I'll see what I can do, sir," she said. "I have friends who dress more colorfully than I. Perhaps I can bring them along. You know perfectly well who they are." She paused. "Perhaps we'll even like her. What is her name?"

"Colorful people are always welcome. They'd counteract your drab dress, Melantha," said DeVille. "I expect you'll all like her. Her name is Cora." After a hungry, lingering look at Cora, he left the room, knowing that it would be some time before he would be so close to her again. There were occasions when he could be disciplined.

Melantha went to the door after DeVille left and gestured to a friend passing by in the hallway to come into the room and sit for a few moments with Cora while she left to improve her appearance. When she returned she wore a yellow sash around her waist. A red scarf adorned her throat. She had washed her face and hands and had combed her hair, and looked less medusan.

Many hours passed before Cora stirred. She gradually roused herself and she slowly opened her eyes. Melantha was sitting slightly behind her so that Cora did not see her at first. Cora looked around at her surroundings. Confused, she pulled herself up to have a closer look. She rubbed her eyes. She could see that she was in a brightly lighted room. But where was she? It was a mystery. Though it was mid-morning, the sun was just beginning to come in through the open windows. A fire burned in a large fireplace and Cora could feel its warmth.

The room had large windows and was furnished with chairs and tables, and carpets. There were pictures on the walls, though she could not see what they were precisely. Her eyes felt blurry, and she was headachy. She turned her head to look behind her, and shrank back when she saw Melantha, saying "Oh!"

Melantha immediately said "Hello, Cora. Don't be afraid. Everything is fine."

Cora, looking straight at Melantha, absorbed her voice and her words. Then, looking around, she burst into tears and said, through sobs, "Where am I? Who are you? Where is my mother? I want my mother. Where am I?"

"Don't be afraid. A friend has brought you here for a little visit. This is a lovely place. Just look at this room. My name is Melantha, by the way."

Cora raised herself up and said forcefully, "I don't care. I don't care what your name is. I don't want to be here. It's not true that a friend brought me here. No friend of mine would do this to me. How did I get here? Was I kidnapped?" She was yelling now. "How dare anyone bring me to some strange place? It's not right! It's not fair! I want to go back to my home and my mother right now. I'm going home right now."

She started to get up, but fell weakly back onto the sofa. Whatever the potion that had been forced on her, its effect had not completely worn off. Cora cried out in dismay. "This is not fair. You are evil keeping me here. Evil! Evil! I demand that whoever brought me here take me back, and right this instant."

Melantha sighed. She thought, "Why am I always given these dirty jobs? I wonder how *this* adventure will end? Well, I think I can guess." She said aloud, "Oh, Cora, I *am* sorry about this too but I fear there's nothing I can do and definitely nothing possible that you can do. I strongly suggest that you try to accept the fact that you've been taken away to where you have no idea, and that neither of us has any idea how long it will last nor what the result will be."

"I can't possibly accept that," Cora yelled angrily at Melantha. "When my mother finds out, you can be sure she *will* move heaven and earth to find me and take me home where I'll be safe, and whoever is responsible for this will surely pay a price. You can be very sure."

At that moment there was a soft knocking at the door and a woman came in carrying a tray with food. She carried elegant juices and warm breads, sweet jams and jellies, and a pitcher of milk. "This is my friend, Rhoda," said Melantha. "She works in the kitchen and loves to bake. You should try some of this food. I'll join you because I'm hungry. I've been up all night watching over you."

"I'm not hungry," said Cora petulantly. But, in fact she *was* hungry and, to be truthful, when she saw Melantha clearly enjoying the bread and jam, and after the aroma of the warm bread had reached into her soul, she couldn't help herself. She reached for the tray. Rhoda quickly took a plate, removed the napkins keeping the bread warm, sliced some pieces, smothered them with jam and jelly, and gave them to Cora. Cora ate hungrily, dropping crumbs she cared not where, and drank a glass of milk.

Cora looked at Rhoda who stood smiling at her. Rhoda wore a red apron over a white dress, a little orange cap perched on her head, and dark red slippers. "I am glad you like what I brought, Miss," she said. "I like to bake."

"There's some flour on your chin, Rhoda," said Melantha, wiping Rhoda's face with a napkin. Cora laughed. "There, that's better," said Melantha, smiling.

"But I am still not happy," said Cora, "and I'm serious about wanting to go home."

After she had eaten, she felt sleepy again and, perhaps against her will, nodded off. Melantha and Rhoda observed her and Rhoda said, "Dear me, here we go again."

Melantha was dozing soundly by the fireplace when Cora wakened. After a moment she oriented herself, put one foot on the floor, and then the other, and, bracing herself by the back of the sofa, stood up. She walked gingerly over to a window, steadying herself on the backs of chairs, and looked out. The day was brilliant with sun, and before her were hosts and hosts of daffodils, acres without end of daffodils. More than she had ever seen. She gasped at the seas of yellow crowding, crowding in upon one another. She had no idea that there could be so many varieties.

The door opened and a tough-looking blond woman came in dressed in yellow and white. Cora could not keep from laughing. "You look just like those daffodils out the window," she said, grinning.

The woman did not smile. "You are not the first one to make that remark, young woman. I have heard it for many years now. I happen to like to wear this color.

"What's this?" she demanded, pointing to Melantha, noisily. At that, Melantha opened her eyes.

"Oh, it's you, is it, Xantippe. I knew you'd have to stop by after you heard that we have such a fine guest. Cora, meet Xantippe. She's a good friend of mine even if she is brusque, and ill-tempered at times."

"Ah, well, I have good reason for my reputation, don't I, the way I'm treated around here!"

"Yes, but it's an old story, isn't it. You're treated that way because you act so badly. You ride roughshod over everything."

"Chicken or the egg?" Xantippe challenged. "Yes, I have a reputation," she said to Cora. "Things just annoy me. So, this is fair warning. Watch out for me, now."

Cora, not knowing how serious Xantippe was, said nothing, but took her advice. She looked closely at Xantippe, listened to her flinty conversation, observing her roughness, her apparent independence, and her "fear-nobody" front. Then, on impulse, daring to experiment because of her own unhappy situation, she spoke. "Xantippe, will you be my friend?"

Xantippe, surprised, looked at her and said through tight lips, "You want me for a friend? We'll see about that. It all depends on how you treat me. Treat me well and you'll not be disappointed." Looking around the room, she abruptly added, "I can see I'm not needed here." She left, just like that, surprised by Cora's request, leaving her with Melantha, who seemed about to return to her nap.

Cora walked about the room and stopped in front of the paintings. One showed a large pastoral scene – a huge evening sky with billows of yellow-tinged late afternoon clouds, noble, gigantic red olive trees, a gentle stygian stream, and a field of wind-belled anemones with striped celandines in the foreground. Two sweet girls with hair like tiny garter snakes huddled together, pointing far into the background of the painting toward barely discernible herds of animals – picturesque animals with the heads of men, and the bodies of goats. The herds to their right had heads and arms of men, with the lower extremities of horses. Still another, barely discernible group grazing in the gathering dark, had the heads of bulls and human torsos.

Another equally excellently executed painting was a three-quarter bust of a demurely smiling sphinx, a scroll marked "riddle" between its paws, with a single pearl dangling from its earlobe. Another painting was of a scene on a wharf, in which entranced sailors were leaning forward, listening to beautiful young women on a ship singing to them. Their graceful arms beckoned the sailors to come aboard. Indeed, some sailors were in the act of boarding the ship, unable to resist.

Finally Cora looked at a very large painting titled "Watch in the Night," a dark painting of vigilant watchmen in the gathering gloom, bearing swords and lances. Banners and lanterns flourished. These were serious creatures, bent on safeguarding the citizens of the city. Among the guardians were armored, fire-breathing, light-providing lion-goats, goat-legged warriors, and rams with the bodies of lions, and a child-horse with a dead chicken at its waist. The artist had portrayed these guardians of the peace marching forward so graphically that Cora stepped back for a moment before realizing that the painting was static, and that she was perfectly safe.

As Cora explored the room, this prison of hers, Xantippe returned. "I have been thinking," she said. "What was that about being friends?" She had just spoken when two other women came into the room. One had the biggest, bluest eyes Cora had ever seen; and she wore a blue apron that complemented her eyes. The other wore green shoes and a green over-blouse.

"You are the most colorful people I have ever seen!" said Cora.

Xantippe said, "We are indeed. But we haven't much choice. It is demanded of us."

"How can that be?" asked Cora. Then she made a guess: "Is it the one who brought me here and has me jailed here?"

"My name is Sian," the blue-eyed woman said, "And this is Chloris. We are here to see if there is anything you need or if there is anything we can do for you."

"What nonsense," said Xantippe. "Sian, you know you just came because you wanted to see the latest arrival. Sian here is in charge of the daffodil gardens. She is a busy person, though she has a large crew. Chloris works with her… when they work, I might add. Scat, you two, or I will fix you for lunch." After inspecting Cora closely, Sian and Chloris brashly sauntered out, bursting into laughter as they closed the door behind them. "What's this about being the 'latest arrival'?" asked Cora.

"Now, what is this about being a friend?" asked Xantippe, ignoring Cora's question.

Cora explained. "I really don't know what made me ask you, though maybe there's something about you that appeals to me. Maybe you understand my situation and maybe you can help me. You appear to be a person with character."

"That I am," said Xantippe. "That I am." Then, "You've been analyzing me, haven't you. But for my part I must tell you that I know nothing about you. That makes it difficult to become friends. Do you understand me?"

"I do," said Cora. "What do you want to know about me?"

"Let me think," said Xantippe. "Here is how we'll start: tell me about what you do on a normal day at home."

"At home? On a normal day?" said Cora. "Let me think." She leaned back and put her feet on a stool. "Well, I spend the mornings in bed, and usually don't get up until noon. I doze off and on, and look out the window to see what kind of day it is and whether the wind is blowing in the trees, and I look around the room at all my things, especially my clothes. Then, about mid-morning, I usually ring the bell by my bed and a maid brings me my breakfast. She waits while I eat and tells me the news of what is happening on the farm and in the village. I like it when calves are born and there is news that there are tinkers prowling about. Hearing that the shopkeepers are quarreling is always enjoyable.

"Then she goes and another maid comes in and we decide what I am going to wear that day. It takes such a long time to decide because I can't make up my mind easily; I have so many clothes. It is mid-afternoon by the time I get dressed, and I am hungry again, so I usually ring to have something else to eat. By that time my friends have gathered downstairs, and they all come up to my room and I send the maid to bring more food, and we sit and gossip. We get really loud sometimes!

"We just talk about local things, of course, because we don't really know anything else and we are not interested in all the things the big people talk about. Sometimes one of the girls brings news of a horse that got out of its stall and is running loose because of some stupid barn-boy, and that gives us a good laugh. Sometimes one of the girls has a new dress and we take turns wearing it. We are all the same size, you know. If anyone gets bigger so she can't wear everyone's clothes, we don't invite her anymore. It's a fact of life.

"Then we usually go for a walk. Sometimes we go to the village and sometimes into the woods nearby and sometimes we go into a field to pick flowers, like I was doing yesterday when I was so rudely taken away. Against my will! We sometimes meet other girls on our walks and we chat with them a little, but after they are gone we talk about them. Some of our girls say the rudest, funniest things!

"In the evenings we all have dinner together, and then they go home and I go to my room and look at the pictures on the walls and watch the big clock tick-tocking. It is so soothing and I like that. By then I am really tired because of the exhausting day, so go to bed. I sleep really well, I can tell you. You can see that I get lots of sleep. I can use it," said Cora.

Xantippe stared at Cora. "Is that what you do?"

"I think that is a normal day, yes."

"Let me see," said Xantippe. "Do you know how to cook?"

"No!" she said in wonder, "What could you be thinking? That's what cooks are for."

"Do you ever make your own bed?" Cora stared unbelievingly at Xantippe.

"How about sewing? Do you know how to sew or to alter clothes?" Cora shook her head slowly. Clearly not.

Xantippe, knowing her questions were futile, asked, "Have you ever dug in the dirt in a garden?"

Cora shook her finger in that universal sign for "no".

Xantippe, desperately seeking some redeeming aspect of Cora that would rescue her from being an absolutely empty-headed, spoiled-rotten brat asked, "What about reading? Do you have books and do you read?"

Cora thought before she responded. "No. Yes, I have books, but I don't read. One of the maids reads to me. But I mostly like stories about little animals and their adventures. Reading can be tiresome."

"So," said Xantippe, preparing to sum up, "You ask me to be a friend, and I'm willing to be your friend if you're willing to let me tell you how I see you. Now, I warn you that a friend is one who's free to say what she thinks, if the other can put up with it and see that it's meant to be helpful."

Cora did not look doubtful for a moment. She had no idea what Xantippe might have in store for her. She smiled a charming smile of smug anticipation and ran her hands through her dark hair and looked sweetly at Xantippe. "Oh, please, please tell me!"

"Young lady, you will not like what I am about to say to you." Cora smiled, incapable of believing that anything negative could be said about her.

"Cora, I find you to be shallow and empty-headed. I also find no possible justification for your being on this earth. What possible good are you to anybody? You only think about yourself."

Cora turned red. She yelled, "You stupid person. You moron. No one who is a friend would say anything like that. I don't want you as a friend. I was wrong about you. Go away! Now!"

Unperturbed, Xantippe challenged her. "Answer me this, Cora. If you were at home, in bed, and rang the bell for food, and no one came, what would you do?"

"What a stupid question. I'd open the door and yell and I'd scream so people would know I was angry, and I would demand that somebody bring me my food."

"And," said Xantippe, enjoying herself, "suppose there wasn't anyone outside the door to answer your screams. What would you do?"

"Naturally, that would never happen," said Cora. But she paused to think. "I would go to the kitchen," she said triumphantly, "and look for some people and some food."

"Do you even know where the kitchen is?"

"*Of course*, I do. Yes, I think so," answered Cora.

"Suppose," said Xantippe, enjoying letting her mind frolic, "suppose that in the kitchen, if you could find it, there was no one there, and suppose that all you could find in the way of food would be some flour and salt and eggs. What would you do?"

"*I do not like these questions!* Stop it," Cora demanded.

"You see, Cora, you are useless. There is no point to you. It is no wonder you were brought here. You are a perfect candidate for… " but there she stopped, unwilling to give away too much of the future.

And Cora, angry, yelling, and crying in her self-centeredness, missed what Xantippe had almost said.

"If you had to sew a tear in your dress you could not mend it. If you had to read the directions on how to open a window it would be beyond you because you read so little."

Cora threw a pillow at Xantippe. "You see what a friend is for? I am a mirror for you to look at and see yourself."

"You can't possibly be a friend. I know what friends are like. I have a lot of friends at home."

"Yes you do. And I will bet that if you didn't feed them all that food and surround them with elegance and indolence that they would stop coming to see you, Little Princess."

"You are cruel. Cruel! Cruel! Cruel!"

"Yes, I am. But just wait. See what I have in store for you. Now stop your blubbering and listen to me. I want to test something about you. Do you hear?"

Cora continued to scream, holding her hands over her ears.

Xantippe went on. "Oh be still, Cora. Cora listen to me. LISTEN! You were looking at those pictures on the wall when I came in, weren't you. No, don't turn around and look at them. Listen to me. I want you to describe the pictures. First, how many are there?"

Cora thought. "Four," she said.

"Good," said Xantippe. "Now, describe them to me."

Cora thought. Still sobbing a little, she said, "There is a big one with lots of people carrying swords and flags."

"Right," said Xantippe. "Go on."

Again Cora concentrated. "And there is one with two girls looking back into the picture. There are lots of clouds. Yellow clouds. Yellow, like you."

Xantippe nodded in approval, glancing back at the picture. "And," Cora went on, "there is one with crowds of people in a place I don't know about."

Xantippe took a look. "Yes, that is right and we will talk about it later. Now, there is one more."

"I don't remember," said Cora. "Help me."

Xantippe looked at the last of the four and said, "It has some writing in it."

"Oh, is it the one with the girl's head and something is dangling from her ear?"

"That's right," said Xantippe, encouraged. She said, "Here, turn around and look at the paintings."

Cora did, then turned and looked at Xantippe. "See?" she said. "Pretty good."

Her inquisitor nodded in agreement, then said, "I have still another test of your memory. Are you ready, young lady?"

"Yes. I suppose."

"Name the women who you have met this morning."

Cora looked around. Melantha and Xantippe were there, so she named them immediately.

"How do they distinguish themselves?" asked Xantippe.

"Easy. Melantha is naturally in black and you are mostly in yellow."

"What about the others?'

"Let me see. One was in red. I remember; her name is Rhoda. Another in blue is named Sian. Is that right? Oh, and her friend was dressed in green and is called Chloris.

"I am amazed," said Xantippe. "Here I said you are useless, and I thought you were a waste of time." Pausing, she stood in front of Cora and placed her hands on Cora's shoulders. Looking Cora straight in the eyes, she said, "but, I have just decided you are worth investing my time, and you'll get out of your predicament when I am through with you. Do you hear me?"

"I hear you, but I don't understand what you are talking about."

"It's a mystery for now. If we are to accomplish the goal which you do not really understand, it will take work on your part. *Work* has not been in your vocabulary. But it will be now. And when we are done, you will be an accomplished young woman, and you will control your own destiny."

Pluto

Tophat DeVille could not have been accurately described as *apoplectic* when he heard the results of the Tri-Partite division, but neither could he have been described as ecstatic. "Diabolic hatred" is more like it. One brother had been given the seas, the other the mountains, and he had been given land. Plain old land. Boring flat land and all that lay beneath it. "My God," he cursed. "What did I do to deserve this?"

How he regretted the loss of the sea. How he loved to scuff along on miles of white sandy beach. How he loved the rocky coasts where the surf battled the fortresses of stone, casting its waters miles high over the battlements to wear them down. How he enjoyed the northern river mouths where the tide stopped great rivers dead in their tracks. How intriguing to be at the equator where the insipid tide groveled its way quietly across the sand. And the islands and atolls, and hot springs rising from hidden volcanoes. The ichythian dolphins and the cetaceous bow sharks. The sea was a never-ending wonder to DeVille, and now it was forever lost to him.

So it was with the mountains he had loved to climb. The ranges. The continent-piercing cordilleras. The monstrous domed outcroppings. The volcanoes, sharp and worn. The lowland foothills and the alpine pastures. Gone. Now they were gone to him, never more to be seen. His was a distinctly undramatic land: the prairies, the veldt, the pampas, the heath, the steppes, the savannas. "O God, help me," he had cried when the decision came.

"You'll come to see the beauty of the land," one brother had said patronizingly while privately thanking the powers that be for his good fortune. "You'll see the beauty of the flowers and the animals and the changes of season."

"Oh, shit," said Tophat DeVille. "Just shit, shit, shit." *Why was he the odd-man out?* he wondered, but there was nowhere to turn, no ear to hear. After the straws had been pulled and his fate decided, he had stayed on in the castle, deferring traveling to his unmerited inheritance, enjoying the company of others. He went hunting with expert huntresses, taking deep pleasure in them. He danced with the amusing artists who occupied space in the castle.

After a month, he noticed that some of his friends had drifted away. "They are away, and the Heavens only know when they will be back," DeVille was told by reliable sources. "Business" took his fortunate brothers away one day. Soon no one was bringing food to his room, and when he went to the kitchen he was given many apologies for this breach of hospitality. One day when no food appeared, he trekked to the kitchen only to find a serving girl sweeping the floor. She did not know much about the food situation, but found him a few crusts of bread and some barely drinkable wine.

There was no dinner that night.

The next day there was no one, absolutely no one around.

Tophat DeVille, deserted and feeling abused, packed up and headed for his territory. He moaned. He bewailed his fate and would not be consoled.

After a long journey to what would become the center of his universe, he arrived at a city set among gentle and not altogether unpleasant rolling uplands. Everyone knew who he was, and all bowed down to him, not daring to presume their fate. He quickly established his authority, having long been schooled in the art of authoritarianism, after having been accustomed to being in control, and after, of course, his disappointment at the outcome.

He learned that the principle industry in this area was mining. Such a mean operation was repugnant to him, until it slowly dawned on him that the earth, the very soil on which he walked was the source of riches. His interest was considerably piqued, for he realized that as sovereign he could become rich.

He thought of his brothers and was amused to think of the advantage in having been given the flatlands. It was one thing to be the ruler of all the mountains and to have a perch on the highest of them, to see all that he surveyed. It was still another to hold sway over the seven seas, over crayfish and kelp. Yet it was something else to become wealthy, gigantically wealthy, indeed a plutocrat.

He began to scheme. He called and appointed advisors, to their great surprise, because no one had ever considered consulting them before that moment. The consultants were happy to consult. Together they planned how to extract more tin and copper and iron and coal. Before long there were underground mines for hundreds of miles in every direction. Tunnels dove deep into the earth. Vast caverns were created and shored up.

After he deigned to visit one of the deep-bored mines, DeVille asked his consultants, "Is there anything that all those underground tunnels can be used for?"

There was much scratching of heads. Then one consultant who was usually courageous enough to express an opinion finally said, "To tell you the truth, I have some relatives who carry their dead deep into an old mine shaft near them. Saves them money."

Instantly DeVille laughed out loud and, addressing the man who had just spoken, said, "That is brilliant! Brilliant! You have just caused me to have the most delicious idea! Thanks to you, and your relatives." He paused to let this introduction sink in. "We will make use of the mine tunnels and caverns as a burial site, the largest in the world, and we'll charge the mourning public for this use. It is a brilliant idea, if I do say so myself.

"This is wonderful," he continued, "it will appeal to the whole world. No more charnel houses. No more potter's fields, no more bone yards and boot hills. We shall make a necropolis, a city of the dead, and all the world will come with their dead. We shall call it The Necropolis, and we shall make a killing."

As the consultants savored the majesty of this idea, a gray-haired consultant said, "Something has occurred to me, Master. This underground burial might not appeal to everyone. What about the wealthy? What of the famous? Shall all be treated the same?"

Tophat DeVille frowned. It was a good point, an excellent point the gray-haired one made. Was this a chance to make even more money? "Let's think about this carefully as we begin to develop The Necropolis," he said.

Some days later the consultants reconvened and began to share ideas. "Remember," said Tophat DeVille didactically, as if looking over the top of his glasses, "all ideas are welcome. Nobody must say anything negative about anybody else's ideas." Never had the consultants encountered such humanity, such openness in a leader. Such a progressive person, they agreed later as they sipped their sea-dark wine.

In the end, through such beneficial group interaction, it was decided they would construct a beautiful burial place on the surface of The Necropolis, and that it would be covered in every direction for miles and miles, and tens and tens of miles with daffodils, perpetually blooming, ever fresh daffodils because they had been Tophat DeVille's favorites from his youth onward.

It would be an uplifting place. Beautiful statues would be raised, architectural wonders would be found at ever turn. No matter that they were really columbaria and mausoleums. Above the tunneled catacombs, dank and dreary and cheap, would be places of light and happiness. There would be no sorrowful obituaries, no mournful epitaphs debasing the headstones. It would be expensive and exclusive. "Ah yes, we scraped together enough to bury Uncle Philip in The Necropolis of Daffodils," would be the elitist watchword. "It's worth every penny."

So, came the architects and landscapers, the surveyors and gardeners, and the workers by the hundreds, and it was so. It was a beauty, and the demand exceeded the hopes of the consultants and of Tophat DeVille himself.

Soon they were sitting pretty, though DeVille sat on top. Now they had riches, though DeVille was by far the richest. The mines of copper and tin and iron and coal, and the burial tunnels below joined to the beautiful places of rest above. Life could hardly be better.

But wait! There is more. One day when the counsel was meeting, one of the counselors came into the room brushing dull, yellowish specks from his coat. Amused, DeVille asked where he had been to become so colorful. "Oh, Sire, have you never been to the Yellow River? It's one of the several rivers that run through The Necropolis, but it's such an irksome place.

"It's called *Yellow* because that is what it is," he continued. "The water is yellow and the banks of the river are the same. Even the ground around the river is yellow. The stuff gets all over. When the ground dries the dust flakes up and gets all over one's clothes and in one's hair. The wind blows and it gets in the lungs. It is hard to avoid swallowing the stuff. I try to stay away from the place, but sometimes that is impossible, as you can see from the way I look. We all hate that ugly river. Nobody likes it."

DeVille's ears perked up. He fingered the man's clothing. Was he hearing what he thought he was hearing? Was it possible that these people had no idea? "Hmm. Tell me more."

The consultant went on. "There's a funny story about that river. Actually, it's about how it came to be in that deplorable condition. The story goes that a very long time ago an old man came to the river with an affliction. Somehow, don't ask me how because I have no idea, somehow this affliction meant that everything he touched turned into that yellow stuff. I mean to tell you that he could not even eat, because the moment food touched his lips it turned hard yellow. Imagine a hard yellow potato! He was frantic because he knew if he didn't eat, he would die. Somehow he had heard that if he were to come to this particular river and bathe in it he would be cured of the affliction.

"And so he came. He traveled a great distance, and by the time he arrived, he was almost dead. He had not eaten nor had anything to drink for a very long time because it was impossible. He had to get to the river by himself since anything he touched, including his servants, were likely to turn yellow and hard as a brick.

"He managed to get into the river and he bathed himself thoroughly, up one side and down the other. When he got out of that useless river, he hoped and prayed he was cured.

"He picked up a brown stick, and it stayed brown! He went off rejoicing and praising the powers above, hopping about, leaping from one foot to another, touching trees and rocks and servants wildly, with none of the former result. It was as if he had received his sight again. He vowed vows all over the place, which nobody understood. Then, the story goes, he drove away, gorging himself on a potato, savoring it as if it were ambrosia.

"But unfortunately he left the river a disgrace. It was transformed into the disgraceful condition it is in now. Such a pretty river it was before this man came; such an awful place now." He brushed more flaky yellowish bits off his cloak.

"I will see this river," said DeVille, scarcely able to control himself. He reached over and took a few of the specks from the man's cloak and examined them in the palm of his hand carefully. "I know that old, old story. You may be in for a surprise. A happy surprise, if I do say so."

Soon Tophat DeVille, with great glee, introduced his naïve, untutored friends to the joys of gold, and the pleasures of being even richer.

Nomads

After cleansing themselves of the odor of the Parliament of Judges, Demi and Sophia sought a place to rest for the night. It had been a long and unsatisfactory day among the black robes. No judge had been deemed the "fairest". Demi and Sophia still had the golden ball, and they were exhausted by the treatment they gave the judges.

With the drumming beating its theme, they settled in for the night in a pleasant grove of sycophant trees. They gathered vast armfuls of wind-blown anemones, and downy acacia plants and piled them under the trees. They feasted on ripe figs hanging invitingly from the sycophant trees, and laughed at each other as fig juice dripped from their chins. They accompanied the figs with white cheese which they had laid by the day before at the trading post. The drumming remained low and steady.

As they settled, rested at last, Sophia, gazing up at the starry night, said, "My dear mistress, I confess that I'm distressed about your village and the people and the fields."

"And as for me, Sophia," said Demi, "I can't think about them. We haven't been gone very long. They'll be all right. I'm concentrating solely on finding Cora and thinking about that beastly brother of mine, Tophat, and what he is up to. We must, must, must find Uncle Theo. That's all that matters! And there's an end to it." She gritted her teeth as she spoke. "We must press on, Sophia. Theo's the key to finding Cora. We must find Theo if we're to have any success in winning Cora's release. I'm furious at him for leading us on this merry chase." Then, stressing every syllable, she said, "I am determined to find him. I do not care about the people or the village or the fields. They can be damned as far as I care!"

"But Demi, for me that's a dilemma," said Sophia sharply, "because both causes are urgent. I care about Cora, but I'm also concerned about our people and what they're going through without us."

For some time Demi stared at Sophia, musing about her and her words. Then decisively she said, "All right. Send Eulie. Eulie will find out what the situation is at home. That'll save us time. We aren't so far from there. If he leaves now he can tell us what he has found in the morning. Now, let's get some rest."

So Eulie was dispatched. It pleased him to be sent off during the night hours, his favorite time, on a mission of such significance. He would be able to use his powers of observation and report fully. He whispered owlishly to Sophia that he might be returning much later than Demi had suggested because he would want to observe how life was proceeding during the day as well as the night. He flew off with her blessing.

After an hour's flight, Eulie landed on a branch of The Great Dendron Tree, and began to look around. It was late afternoon, and there was a misty darkness in the air. Such was the atmosphere that there was no chance for moon nor stars, and not, of course, for any sun to penetrate.

Feeling hungry after his flight, he looked about and he saw mice lying lethargically below the tree. Eulie dined well. He continued his night watch, but nothing was moving.

Morning came. It was only the fourth morning since Demi, Sophia, Eulie, and Cynique had left on their search for Cora. The sun came up, but it peeked out far later than usual, and Yellowpants arrived, far, far later than usual, and climbed the tree as per custom, but was more confused than ever by the heavy mist and the sun's brief appearance. That was the day he gave up coming. So disquieted was he, so disoriented, that he who sees all did not even notice Eulie in the tree.

Those few villagers who ventured out were mystified after days of diminishing sunlight. The cows and sheep looked about confused, expecting some attention, some comfort from their masters. But there was none. A general malaise, a somnolence had set in. Eulie felt himself becoming listless. but he dismissed it, thinking, "Isn't it usual for an owl to rest during the daylight hours?" Still, it occurred to him, he had best stay awake, because he had his report to make. Even so, despite his resolve, he felt himself growing lethargic. He was filled with the sense that he might be overcome. He took hold of himself. "This is strange. This is not right. I must rouse myself. I have work to do."

It was with some effort that he raised his wings, and forced himself to jump from the branch, determined to fly. He swooped, but fell, pulled by a force stronger than gravity, out of control. But Eulie was determined. By what grace he could not guess, he swung around and began an upward climb. With pure grit he straightened himself out and gained altitude and was in his element. Exultant, he began to do the job he had been assigned. With his sharp sense of hearing and his ability to see through the heavy grayness, he became acutely aware of what was happening all around. He confirmed that all was dullness below. Few, neither man nor beast, were out and about. Those who moved did so as if shackled by Promethean chains.

Eulie circled Demi's vast property for hours, observing, observing, all the time fighting the impulse to give in to the enervating, slaty morass. It became harder and harder. But at last, thanks to pluck and owlish gymnastics, he soared high into the clean air and the sunshine, free of the snare. He circled the property twice, enjoying the sun and the blessed clean air and his recovered energy, then headed back, in search of Demi and Sophia and Cynique, amusing himself by thinking about what the atmosphere would be among them.

When Eulie found the three, they had gone a day's march, following the ephemeral signs that Uncle Theo had casually cast about. When Eulie spied them, they were climbing a ridge, following lengthy switchbacks. At each turning point of the switchbacks lay mounds of crazed schizoids, placed to keep night travelers from losing the trail. They stopped frequently to rest and, whether Demi wanted to do so or not, they took time to admire the view.

"My, it is beautiful," said Sophia.

"Yes, I suppose it is," replied Demi. "Let's keep on." Just then, a small herd of yellow long-horned monopods came crashing down the trail, forcing Demi and Sophia to fall hard against the hillside. Cynique, who stared in disbelief at the beasts, uncomprehending, started to run down the trail, but was bowled off the path by them. He tumbled down to the path below, but quickly recovered his balance and climbed back up to Demi and Sophia. "Another of Theo's signs," said Demi. "That one was not a nice one," she added.

"Wait a moment," said Sophia, "the golden ball fell out of my pocket when I took that tumble. Oh, there it is."

They had stopped for a bite when Eulie arrived. "Where have you been?" asked Sophia sternly.

"I told you that I would not be back early because I needed to observe what was happening during the daylight," Eulie replied indignantly.

"Report," ordered Demi.

Eulie jumped onto Sophia's shoulder. He preened his feathers and looked about, twisting his head in all directions. He settled in as a hen settles on a nest, and began. "Since you have left, the sun has disappeared. Now there is only a heavy gray mist. This sudden change has left the people distraught, and the sheep and cows and the other animals unsettled, for life is not the same.

"I overheard many conversations, and they all have come to the same conclusion, that it is your absence which is the culprit. They believe that life is dying out. Even faithful old Yellowpants has given up. He stays at home staring into the fireplace, a miserable substitute for the sun, which, of course, is at the heart of his life. To say that he is depressed and that the others are dispirited is to vastly understate the situation. Animals included.

"There's a great grayness which has settled over the whole area. It's unhealthy, it's miasmic. To breathe it is to fall into the same malaise."

Eulie's report had a dampening effect on Demi and Sophia. "I knew it," said Sophia.

"What do you mean 'you knew it'?" retorted Demi. "You knew no such thing. How could we have known what would happen?" She paused, almost sheepishly, remembering Sophia's abilities. She turned and faced Sophia, Eulie, and Cynique. "Still," she said recouping, "we must carry on. We'll not be long. I feel it. We must see to saving Cora from DeVille. Let's go!"

In an hour they had reached the top of the ridge and wondered what to do next. The low persistent beat of the drums intensified as they stood trying to decide. Before them lay a split in the trail; one branch ran along the ridge, and the other headed downward. Sophia studied it, for she loved such crossroads. "There!" she shouted, "That's the way." She pointed toward the downward trail where a little shepherd girl, bearing an armful of amaryllis, was leading three lambs.

They gathered their belongings, preparing to descend in that direction. When they looked for the girl farther down the path, she was nowhere to be found. "This is definitely the way to go," declared Demi. "That was Uncle Theo at work." The girl was indeed gone, but what was coming into view was a deep, brilliantly lighted valley, gleaming even as night began to fall. *"What is this?"* thought Demi, and she ordered Cynique and

Eulie to race ahead and see what they could see. Demi and Sophia started down.

From their vantage point, they could see a vast valley through which a river ran. Several villages or settlements were visible, the largest lay directly below them. It was a vision of white. The cattle, the cultivated fields, all were brilliantly white. The steep-sided mountains on either side of the valley were filled with white-barked poplar and aspen.

It was not long before Cynique and Eulie returned. It is an amazing valley, they reported, filled with people and several villages, actively going about life as one would expect. All normal in every respect except for one thing, everything is white. White, white, white. The people are white. The animals are white; the houses are white; the grass and the trees are white. The hair on the heads of the people is white. And it all shines. *Who,* wondered Sophia and Demi, *are these people? Where are we?*

Pyrotechnics

Xantippe came calling on Cora early the next morning. "Get up, my girl, we have work to do."

Before long, Cora found herself in the kitchen, standing before a large bowl of flour. "Today you are going to learn how to make bread." Cora was astonished. Xantippe continued, "You wonder why, don't you, my girl. This is the first step in your education. If you don't understand fundamentals of life, you can hardly be said to be educated. Do you know what the word *fundamental* means, Child? You are about to grow up. Do you know what that means, Child?"

Cora's education began with learning to mix flour and water just so, and to add a little salt and leavening, then to roll out the dough and form a thin, flat, round shape, and then to put it in a hot skillet. She learned the painful lesson of turning over the bread with the tips of her fingers. She learned to make bread with more ingredients. She began to enjoy mixing the dough with her hands, and the anticipation of pulling the bread from the oven, and the taste of newly baked, warm bread. "See what I made!"

One day when Xantippe came to rouse Cora, she was gone. Xantippe found her in the kitchen already working on bread, using different flours and experimenting with placing the dough in boiling oil. "Are you using a recipe for that, Cora?" she asked.

"No. I am making it up. This is delightful."

Soon she added, "Xantippe, as I was walking here this morning, I thought I saw a man watching me. Maybe he was following me too, though I couldn't quite see."

"Ah," said Xantippe, "Was he tall, with a beard? Was he elegantly dressed?"

"I think so, though I couldn't tell you with any certainty."

"I'll deal with him," said Xantippe, angrily. "But I tell you one thing: you are not to go about alone. You should have awakened Melantha and had her bring you here. She will be wondering where you are, if she's not still in bed, the lazy woman."

In fact, at that moment Melantha, her black clothing swirling about her, came rushing in.

"Oh, there you are, Child! You know you are not supposed to go anywhere without me."

"I am sorry, Melantha, but I must be about my education, don't you see?"

As Cora was mastering bread-making, Xantippe taught her the basics of bread and its role in civilizing the world. She taught her about water – Cora's knowledge being abysmal – of the forms it can take, from steam to ice, of how all forms of life need water to exist, of the wars fought over water, and, holding nothing back, how water can be used in torture, and finally, how together, bread and water can sustain life, for a while.

Xantippe's education included reading. Cora could read, but did not have the habit. She had to sound out the words she did not recognize and found herself with "Aha!" moments, and with "So, that's how that word is spelled" moments. Over a long period, Xantippe gave Cora interesting stories. She gave her books on how to do things and what things are and what things used to be. She introduced her to life, to reality. Cora came to be a good student and soon read so avidly that Xantippe had to tear her away from her books to move on to other aspects of her education.

Late one evening Cora was lying in bed in her room reading a book on flowers. Her attention had been particularly drawn to a description of a flower's reproductive organs – its stigma, petals, anthers, and sepals. She read the description and looked at the illustrations over and over again. But her reverie was broken by the faintest of noises. She saw the door to her room was opening, and there, to her profound surprise Cora saw a man standing in her room. He was tall, bearded, and elegantly dressed. She shrank back and pulled the covers over her. "Who are you?" she shrieked.

"I'm a friend," he said smiling, and moving closer. He pulled up a chair and sat beside her. He sat and stared at her, studying her, as Cora sat huddled in the farthest corner of the bed, protecting herself with sheets and blankets.

Finally, the man spoke. "Cora, my dear, my name is Tophat DeVille, and I happen to be the owner of all this." He gestured nonchalantly in a way to indicate that everything in every direction, beyond the room, far beyond the room, was his. "This is my house, and this is my room, and everything you see here, including the bed you are sitting on, is mine. And in truth, my very dear, you are mine, too. Do you see that?"

Cora understood what he had said, but was shocked by his assertions. But she said nothing. Tophat DeVille continued to look at her. He wet his lips with his tongue. His hands continually opened and shut. He sat leaning forward, as if to reach out and touch her. The smile on his face made Cora wary. Finally, still staring at her, Tophat said, "I'll be going now. I am glad to have made your acquaintance. I promise you that I'll see you again, and you and I will become very well acquainted." He left the room, as softly as he had come in, closing the door behind him.

After a moment Cora tore out of bed and ran to the door yelling "Melantha." Melantha was sleeping soundly. Cora shook her and shook her, until finally she was roused. "Melantha! Melantha! There was a man in my room who said his name was Tophat. What was he doing there? How dare he come in? Did you let him?"

Melantha, battered by the questions and Cora's screams, trying her best to focus, put her fingers in her ears and finally, in her best drill sergeant manner said, "Be still, Cora! Just shush and sit down. Down!" Gradually Cora stopped her frenetic behavior. "Now Cora," said Melantha, "Did that man do anything to you? Did he touch you in any way? Tell me!"

"No, he didn't do anything but sit and stare at me. He told me his name and said he would see me again. He said that I belonged to him. How can anyone belong to anyone?" She broke into tears, saying "He said that we would soon become much better acquainted."

Melantha was relieved. She stood with her hand over her heart, as if protecting herself from dying, and doubtless also thinking of what Xantippe would say when she heard of the incursion.

Melantha insisted on knowing every detail of the visit, and made Cora repeat what had happened. Then she asked Cora to repeat the details again and again, until she had a clear picture and was sure that Cora had not left anything out, and, if truth be known, that Cora was not making it up.

The next day Xantippe met with Cora. She was blunt. "Cora, Tophat is everything he said he is and more. What he said is true. I gather that modesty prevented him from mentioning how wealthy he is; he is a plutocrat, if there ever was one. But there is more to the story: he is the very one who kidnapped you and brought you here."

Cora's wide eyes blossomed with tears. Thinking of what Tophat had said about her being his, she connected instantly to what she and her friends at home giggled about in whispers, but were innocent of. "What does he want of me?" she asked softly.

Xantippe, her face hard, said, "He wants you for his wife." Cora, her sudden suspicions confirmed, erupted into fountains of tears. Xantippe, unaccustomed as she was, folded Cora into her arms and sat rocking her gently, whispering, "Shh, shh, my little one. Shh."

Cora asked still sobbing, "But why does he want me? He's an old man. Doesn't he have a wife?"

Soothingly as she could Xantippe said, "Yes, Cora, he has a wife. In fact he has lots of wives. You have met some of them. Rhoda and Melantha…"

"And Sian and Chloris? And you, too, Xantippe?"

"Yes. It is true. But we are just a few among many."

"Surely, that is enough," said Cora. "Why does he need me?"

"Tophat DeVille," she said, running her hand soothingly through Cora's hair, "has an eye for young women. And he never has enough. He is always on the search for more. I don't doubt that he had been watching you for a long time, until he considered you old enough. He thinks you are beautiful, and he wants you."

"He kidnapped me!"

"Yes, that's the way he works. That's how we all came here."

"So I would be his wife?"

"Yes, that's the way he works."

"Are you all his wives? Are you married to him?"

"*Wives*, my dear, is a euphemism. Do you know what a euphemism is?" Cora was obviously uncertain. Xantippe explained, "It's a way to improve something by giving it a better name."

"And," said Cora, "wives is a better word for what?"

Xantippe thought. "Servants," she said. "Personal servants."

"Oh," said Cora. "Oh." She stared at Xantippe as she imagined what it was all about. She remembered again what she and her friends had giggled about many times in the quiet of her room.

"I think I know," she said. She looked down at the floor, avoiding looking at Xantippe. "It has something to do with sex, doesn't it?" Xantippe nodded, a yellow scarf flipping back and forth on her head.

"Yes, it does, Cora." Xantippe hastened to add, "But I will help you. There is little we can do about what is inevitable, but I will help you to be prepared, and I think we will find that you will be in charge, if you continue to be a good student in this academy of ours. You will be schooled well."

Xantippe continued, "DeVille is not to be trusted. He will have his way, and he will use any trick to get his way. He promised that he would take his time about getting to know you so you would be used to him, but he lied. He is hungry; so he could not wait. But now that you know who he is and what he desires, you can be in charge. You will control him. He will not trick you. You will use your mind as well as your obvious charms to control him. You will win him over."

"I am petrified, Xantippe."

"Pish! No fears for you, Cora. No trepidations. No dread. No phobias for you. You will win this battle, and I feel there will be consequences unlike any seen around The Necropolis for a very long time."

"Xantippe, there is something I have to ask you. I don't know much about… well… sex. But I know that babies come from it.

How can I say this? What about Tophat DeVille and all of you. Do you have babies? Children?"

Xantippe laughed and laughed. She took Cora in her arms and hugged her and said, "Oh, dear no. No! No! No! None of his wives do, because DeVille has been around The Necropolis and the dead so long that he is absolutely one hundred percent infertile. He is as sterile as a post. It's quite a relief. Can you imagine what any children of his would be like? It's too comical to think about."

"It *is* a relief," said Cora, partly understanding what Xantippe giggled about.

Then, frowning, Xantippe said, "Now, that doesn't mean that DeVille is incapable of… how shall I put it… incapable of sex." She paused. "He's not *impotent*. There, I said it."

"I see," said Cora.

"Come. We don't have much time, now that Tophat has made this move. He'll be considering his next move, and we must be prepared," said Xantippe. "We must go on the offensive."

As time passed, Cora, highly motivated, continued her schooling. She was an apt pupil. She easily absorbed her lessons. She was able to see connections and to derive consequences.

Cora was given lessons in psychology and biology. She studied Demosthenian rhetoric, and diplomacy and calisthenics. Geography and mathematics. She displayed tendencies toward polyglotism and mastered the techniques of art through the paintings on her walls. Music and drama were on the agenda, as was philosophy. In sum, Cora became a polymath, seemingly in preparation for Tophat DeVille.

Xantippe observed one day, "I'm amazed at you. I deemed you useless when you first came. But now I am amazed at you and your learning."

"It's quite so, Xantippe," said Cora. "The truth is that I know far more about a world of things than you do."

"Yes, you do," answered Xantippe. She paused and looked at Cora and said, "Cora, I've been meaning to tell you that it looks like you need some new clothes. That dress just doesn't fit you anymore. See how tight it is? Look in the mirror."

Cora looked and indeed the dress was pulled tight across her body. "Yes, I can see that, but I'm used to it."

Xantippe said, "We need to have some new clothes fitted for you which show off you and your beautiful shape. I'll send in Sian tomorrow. She loves to sew."

In the company of a virtual armada, Cora went outdoors wearing spectacular new clothes and roamed The Necropolis. Now, biologically inspired, she eagerly peered into a daffodil to see if she could find the sepals, the anthers, the pistils and the stamens in the flower. She did. She blushed.

Xantippe was pleased at Cora's precocious analytical abilities and declared her ready for her encounter with Tophat DeVille. "But, Cora, we are going control the situation. First, we shall invite him to a dinner that you yourself have prepared."

"I shall be the cook?"

"Yes, for we'll assure him that you are no ordinary woman, no innocent, untutored, inexperienced woman. And this'll be the first that we'll demonstrate to him. He'll have far more to learn about you before… the inevitable."

"The inevitable?"

"Yes, for he will indeed take you for his wife, Cora. But, Cora, it will be on your terms. Let me assure you."

Cora was numb. But at last she said, "What about this meal?"

"Ah, now, that's better, my lamb, that's better. We'll make discreet inquiries about his favorite foods, and you'll prepare some dishes. We'll overwhelm him."

So, Tophat was invited to dine with Cora. Xantippe and Melantha were to be present as sympathetic minders.

Soon Tophat DeVille's favorite dishes had been spied out by a number of his wives. Xantippe, Melantha, and Rhoda (the baker) huddled over the menu.

They decided on hadean stew rife with ginger and mint, eucalyptus scented nectar, ambrosia a la agave, octopus bits basted in basil and sesame flour, and, for dessert, mystery angel cake with hints of geranium pods. There would be anise flavored drinks, of course.

Melantha suggested, "Let's have some quiet music just outside the room. Guitar and zither would be nice. Adds an ethereal tone, don't you agree?"

The invitation to Tophat DeVille was issued, and accepted. The meal was prepared. Cora actually did have a hand in most of the dishes. The table was set for four, and DeVille arrived precisely on time. He sat across from Cora, who was dressed in a gown which sweetly cloaked her shapely self. As planned, Melantha and Xantippe were also seated. They kept the dishes flowing, while Cora, displaying a newly found self, enthusiastically took the lead in the conversation. Xantippe smiled approvingly.

"Mr. DeVille, I take it from what I have seen all around here that you have a profound interest in daffodils and other related plants. How did that come about?"

Tophat was startled at this display of hosting on the part of one he had considered an untutored, self-absorbed bumpkin, despite having been advised ahead of time. He answered expansively, managing to add that in his travels abroad, as he put it, he often sought out specimens as yet unknown to him. Cora asked him questions about the propagation of the flowers and cross-pollination. And when he acted surprised, she responded that it was a subject about which she had some basic knowledge and which she eagerly desired to explore in depth.

He said, "I'd be happy to give you a tour of the greenhouses where experiments on daffodils are always underway." She gladly accepted.

His mentioning travels led Cora to ask Tophat which of the places where he had visited had most caught his imagination. He named two or three, then appeared dumbfounded when she asked about the economic bases of those places, whether they were based on agriculture or manufacturing, or if they were maritime-based? "And what about the systems of government found there?" she asked.

Tophat harrumphed and said that he hardly had time to investigate such matters. Hoping to gain an advantage, he was just at the point of asking Cora what she had been reading of late, but realized it would be distinctly to his disadvantage. Instead he asked about the food.

"Oh, you're enjoying the food, are you, Mr. DeVille?"

"I am, indeed. The hadean stew certainly hits the spot."

"We thought you might like it," said Cora. "My friends here, as I believe you know, gave me great assistance. They seem to be intimately acquainted with many of your tastes, so we worked out this menu. Frankly, much of it is new to me. I was ecstatic when I first discovered many of these spices. The very smell of them! The flavors! I fear that the food where I come from is bland in comparison.

"Oh, but if you don't mind my changing the subject," said Cora, looking straight into Tophat's eyes and not waiting for an answer, "I have a question. Do you happen to be acquainted with my mother? Her name is Demi. She's quite well known, you know. Oh yes, and my sister, Sophia. Do you know them? I wouldn't be surprised if you did."

Xantippe's and Melantha's heads shot up. Xantippe's arm knocked over her glass of nectar. Their faces turned red. In an instant they were on their feet heading out the door. Never would they have dreamed that their charge, as well educated and confident as she now was, would be so forward, would have such nerve when face to face with Tophat DeVille. Before their unsuspecting eyes Cora had more than flashed into life. It was as if a cold marble statue had, through some magical metamorphosis, become a brash, living damsel, a Galatea come to life.

"Do you know them?" she repeated

"Ah," said Tophat, his mind racing to gain control of the conversation after the unforeseen questions and after the flurry of the women's reaction. Watching the two just closing the door behind them, and knowing precisely what the matter was, he said, "Now, just let me think for a moment." Then, after a momentary pretense at reflection, he shook his head and said with a kindly smile, "No. I'm quite sure I do not." He knew better than to follow through on this line of thought.

Instead, he continued, "You know, my dear, I'm feeling a bit tired. All this good food and exceptionally fine company has made me a bit woozy. It's getting late, and I've some work to do in the office yet tonight, and tomorrow I have an early day. With your permission, I'll excuse myself. This has been an excellent meal, a most pleasant and stimulating hour."

Cora exclaimed in deep disappointment, "But you haven't tasted the dessert we prepared especially for you. It's Mystery Angel Cake. You'd love it." But DeVille demurred. More tantalized by Cora than ever and intrigued by the challenges the changes in this young woman presented, he quickly departed, as an ancient document puts it, "until another time."

Phosphoros

Demi, Sophia, Cynique, and Eulie continued their way down the trail heading toward the valley floor. As if hypnotized, as if it were beyond their control, they seemed to have been drawn toward the aura of brightness. The distant drums beat a sharp tattoo.

As the four neared the entrance to the valley, Sophia suddenly said, "I have a feeling that it would be better if Cynique and Eulie were to hide."

Demi agreed. "Cynique," she said, "stay out of sight, but keep an eye on us. Follow along with us, stay parallel to us, but keep out of sight. Be on the alert, though I certainly fear nothing; this is unknown territory. Eulie, watch us from the tips of the trees."

Eulie hooted softly in Sophia's ear, "Indeed," then flew almost to the top of an aspen and by a fine chameleon's trick, turned white.

"Hmm," said Sophia, learned as she was, she had never seen Eulie do that trick before.

With Cynique and Eulie monitoring them discreetly at a distance, Demi and Sophia descended the path until it ended at a narrow road into the valley of the white.

Hardly had they stepped onto the path, with the village in view, when two armed people stepped smartly out into the road before them. "Halt!" they said.

The two were clad completely in white, which matched the color of their hair and their skins. The only indication of color about them was their narrow, squinchy eyes. One had blue eyes, and the other had black eyes.

Demi and Sophia found it hard to determine just who or what it was they were looking at. It was only their weapons that distinguished them from each other. One carried a spear and a shield, and the other a heavy shield-shaped mirror.

Demi observed, "What a strange weapon. A mirror?"

But Sophia, the wise, immediately grasped the purpose and said, with no little admiration, "Of course! It is used to blind the enemy. How clever. How useful."

"Who are you and what do you want here in the Valley of the Phosphoros?" asked the guards.

"We're weary travelers in these parts. We mean no harm," answered Demi. She and Sophia had pulled themselves in, adopting the ordinary, mousey look they had used when they first entered the Parliament of Judges. "We're simply traveling through and saw your remarkable valley from up on the mountain. Since we're naturally curious, we decided to investigate. We always love to learn about everything new, so here we are," she alibied in the most unprovocative tone of voice she could muster.

"So you say," said the spearholder. "We shall see. Follow us." With the mirror-bearer in the lead and the spearman taking up the rear, they marched their captives off triumphantly. Demi and Sophia soon found themselves shielding their eyes.

The valley was as Cynique and Eulie had reported. A nearly blinding atmosphere surrounded them. The houses and their roofs were white. The streets were of purest alabaster. The trees on the steep hillsides were permanently frosted. The garden flowers were, every single one of them, snowy – alyssum, calla, azaleas, iola, kloris, orchids, and lotus – botanical ingenuity on display.

And so it was with the many people who stood in small clusters and stared open-mouthed at the little procession. Each was a picture in white. Only the color of their narrow eyes distinguished them. Children and naked babies were snow-white. Only by a careful look at their faces could age differences be seen. Indeed, some older people crowded behind others, while others of the older people stood bravely in front shielding the young. None of those who stared knew quite what to make of Demi and Sophia.

Up the street the four marched until they reached a building marked "Archonery". "Here," said the mirrorman, speaking for the first time, "is where our Archon lives. That means that he is the chief."

Sophia hissed, "I know perfectly well what that means. What a pedant."

"Hold your tongue, Sophia," said Demi. "All seems well for now."

The spearman paused before the door and tapped gently three times with the butt of his spear. There was a pause, and then the door opened. Two persons appeared. Just who or what they were, or what gender, or what age they were, was impossible to determine.

They were followed by a tall and aristocratic-looking being who strolled unperturbed into the street, moving closer until he stood nose to nose with Demi and Sophia.

He looked Demi and Sophia up and down. He circled about them. Unabashedly, he delicately touched their clothing. He peered closely into their eyes. He gently stroked their hair. Then he smelled his fingers.

At length, ending his inspection, he turned and gazed expectantly at the spearman and the mirrorman.

"They are intruders, O Mighty Archon."

"I can see that."

"We found them at the edge of the village where we stood guard. They seemed about to enter into our territory. We ordered them to follow us and we have brought them to you."

"I can see that," said the Archon. He looked at the guards. "Tell me, noble guardsmen, how long have you stood guard at the edge of the village?"

"Why sir," said the mirrored one, "perhaps for ten years."

"Then this must be a joyous day for you," replied the Archon. "I believe this is the first time you have ever brought any strangers to me. Tell me, what did they say they were doing, coming into this place?"

"I believe, and my companion can confirm it, as well as these two strangers, that they said, 'We are weary travelers.'"

Sophia added, "And we added that 'we mean no harm.'"

The Archon looked dumbfounded as if affronted that one of the prisoners should dare to speak without permission. Demi misunderstood his look.

"We are not animals," snapped Demi, "We can speak."

"Ah," said the Archon, "I can see that." He continued to stare at them, more intrigued than ever. Demi thought that, if it were possible, he looked paler and paler with every passing minute.

The Archon looked directly at Demi and Sophia, studying them again, then said slowly with a sigh of understanding, "Weary travelers, where are you going? Have you a destination?"

Demi responded. "We seek my daughter. She has been kidnapped. We are sure we know where she is, but we must find the one who can free her, and he is, I must say, leading us on a merry chase."

"I understand," replied the Archon. "And may I know the name of the person whom you seek who leads you on a merry chase? Perhaps I can help."

"Yes," said Demi. "Certainly. It is Theo. He is my Uncle Theo. Theo. A great man with immense powers, but a whimsical person, if I may say so."

"Theo," he replied, rolling the word around in his mouth as one might do while deciding whether it had a familiar taste to it. "Theo. Theo. Hmmm. I fear I don't know him. He sounds like someone I might like to be temporarily acquainted with. In passing, as it were."

"Indeed," said Demi. "The truth is that we are standing here before you precisely because he led us to you. And it appears that you are part of our quest."

"I can see that," said the Archon. "Go on."

"I am beginning to think…." said Demi.

"And so am I," said Sophia, who knew what Demi was about to say.

"I am beginning to think," said Demi, "that there is some purpose in this odyssey of ours. It may be that our visit here will have some effect on us, and possibly that our visit here, no matter how short or how long, may have an effect on you and your people."

"Oh," said the Archon, smiling, the corners of his mouth turned down. "Oh, I doubt sincerely that you will have any effect on us. We are already complete. We are already pure, and there can not be anything purer than pure. We are not subject to change. If I may say so modestly, we are paragons."

Sophia marveled at his egoism.

"However," added the Archon, aware of their disbelief, "I believe you will benefit from your visit with us."

"Oh, sir," Demi added, "we do want to learn here in our brief stay. Sir, may I make a modest request of you?" Seeing the slight bow the Archon made, she continued. "May we prevail upon you to show us how you live? It is part of our quest as travelers to learn the ways of others." There was another slight bow from the Archon. "There is one other thing to ask, if I may. It is this: as it is now late in the day, we will need some shelter and a morsel of food. Is that possible? We are comfortable spending the night under the shelter of trees. It is not difficult for us. Perhaps you would be so kind as to indicate a place which would not inconvenience you."

"With pleasure," said the Archon. He beckoned to one of the two who had come out of the Archonery with him. "This is the village Presbyter, a wise elder. He will guide you and see that you are provided for. Now I must leave you. Urgent business awaits me concerning certain purity issues."

The Archon disappeared into the house and the Presbyter stepped forward. "Come. We will walk in the village and you will see us and hear about us. This village, as you may have heard, is called Phosphoro, and we who live here are the Phosphoros. There's a nice glow to the name, don't you think? But let us walk to the place where you entered the village and begin again."

What the Archon had said about the purity of the Phosphoros was true for him and the villagers. It was their sincere belief, their self-description, that their situation was utopian. For them, their bodies, their very beings had achieved a perfection of whiteness. They were self-sufficient; they were at one with the Sun, the author and giver of life. Here was true paradise. How could one be happier? It was true that their lives were short because, in the end their milky, anemic selves were unhealthy, no matter what they pretended. Yet they contented themselves with the belief that the Elysian fields of the life to come could hardly surpass that which they were experiencing now.

As they walked, the Presbyter explained that there was no evil to be found among them. Kindness prevailed. They had little if anything to fear. The gates of their villages were guarded day and night from outside contamination. The concept of good and evil did not exist among them in this their life together. The Presbyter, enunciating slowly, his voice raised so that the foreigners would understand him better, said "As you can see, our pride and joy, our source of being, is light and the color white, though some say white is not a color. I prefer not to quibble.

"It is not necessarily easy to maintain this whiteness. We spend a great deal of time cleaning and polishing and in applying new paints. Our botanists are expert at breeding color out of the plants so that they, like us, are pure."

"As you can see from the witness of the people we pass, we are happy. We have no cares. We are safe and secure. We have interesting entertainments to occupy our time."

So he guided them through Phosphoro. At last he took them to a house he chose at random. "Come in here," he said. He spoke to the people in the house, saying, "Provide them with food, for they are weary from traveling and they are our guests. I'll return shortly."

"With great pleasure," came the answer, and within a short time Sophia and Demi were seated at a table filled with excellent food. There were plates of white beans and pale fish, bleached broccoli with a silverish gravy, the lightest looking bread they had ever seen, with blanched butter on the side. Ice water stood in large vessels at the ready, and when all was done, they were presented with a dessert of albus cake made with snow-carrots.

It was the most food that Sophia and Demi had eaten for several days, and when they finished, they were happy to lean back contentedly.

Just then the Presbyter came in and said, "Come! You must join us. We Phosphoros are heliocentrics and it is nearly time to bid goodnight to the Sun."

Immediately he left, and their hosts quickly left the house. Sophia, still seated at the table, looked quizzically at Demi. "This certainly must be important," she said.

They followed the crowd which came pouring out of their houses and shops and fields, from the butcher's and the smithy, from every direction in the village, chatting amiably as they went. They were walking with urgency toward the other end of the village from which Sophia and Demi had entered. Sophia and Demi found that everyone was strolling up a slightly elevated patch of ground. All stood on this raised spot with their backs to the village and looked toward a sharp V-shape at the end of the valley ahead of them. Sophia and Demi stood on the fringes of the crowd.

"Long ago we created this little rise you are on," said someone to Demi and Sophia. "It took many years to carry the dirt and construct this little hill, so that we could stand even higher to bid farewell to the Sun. It means we can see the Sun for a minute or so longer. We call it the Farewell Hill."

Someone else added, "Sometimes people go up on the side of the hills to prolong the sad pleasure of seeing the Sun disappear. But though they see it longer, they miss the camaraderie of the rest of us here on the hill saying our goodbyes, so they seldom repeat the climb. Some people like to look up above the V to the sunlight in the trees high above. That light lasts the longest."

They watched the Sun settle down into the V as it had precisely for eons. As the Phosphoros watched it sink down, down, down, there came low mourning goodbyes from them all, a melancholy sound, which increased in intensity as the Sun sank.

Their habit of bidding farewell to the Sun each evening did not symbolize fear of loss (no matter their keening, fond farewells) so much as an honoring of their source of life and the beginning of well-earned rest for themselves and the Sun. They had no such ceremony welcoming their Sun in the morning, for they were simply content to awaken and find their god in his heaven and know that all was right with the world.

When it was gone, the villagers hurried back in silence to their homes, for the dark was coming quickly upon them, and they sought shelter and safety. Stout men appeared to light pyracanthine lamps along the streets, and boys came out of the houses with matches to light giant fraxinella bushes in front of their houses. The bushes gave off a low, soft light all night long, and added a measure of comfort to the neighborhood, fending off the dark.

Their guide, the Presbyter, took them to a quiet place just off the village square, where they might spend the night beneath a snowy diasporal bush, lying on the soft seed pods of a frosted porphyrial tree.

"I hope you will be comfortable here," said the Presbyter. He gestured toward the village. "As you can see, things quiet down rapidly after sundown.

"The only time when there is any appreciable activity here at night," he continued, "is when there is moonlight, but only when there's enough light to see by. Some of our people are enchanted by the 'little Sun', as they call it. Oh yes, and there are those who find a certain amount of excitement in lightning. They are thrilled by the way flashes can light up the clouds. But there are very few admirers, because the storms and noise frighten most of our people. Tonight, however, it appears, will be a quiet and utterly dark night, so there will not be much activity, I can guarantee you."

Then the Presbyter left Demi and Sophia on their own. When the last of the daylight had gone and darkness overlay them,

Cynique appeared from the woods, nudging his head under Sophia's hand, in the way of dogs everywhere, so she would pet him.

Eulie landed on Sophia's shoulder, aloof and self-satisfied, but content to be there, for they had been apart longer than either Eulie or Cynique deemed proper. Eulie was still dressed in white plumage.

Demi whispered to Sophia. "What did you think of what the Archon had to say about these people? Isn't there something admirable about them?"

Sophia said without hesitating, "I'm never too fond of those who have high opinions of themselves. I find it hard to believe that they are such paragons of virtue and living. Something about them stirs up disbelief in me."

Sophia's attention was suddenly turned to the square. She pointed and said, "Look! Look!"

Demi stared in the direction that Sophia pointed saying, "What? What is it? I don't see anything."

Sophia answered, "Look! Look! Don't you see? There are slabs of ice crashing through the village. Stay back! Get out of the way! They're coming our way!"

There before them were monstrous chunks of ice, great glaciers of ice, mountainous bergs of ice, twisting and turning and bashing each other fearfully, gnarling dogs, eating up the square, and furiously carrying with them trees and statues and houses and screaming people toward the end of the village.

Sophia turned for an instant to look at Demi who was not seeing what it was that had Sophia excited. "Over there! Over there!" she pointed. But when Sophia turned back, there was nothing. Absolutely nothing.

"Did you see it? All the ice and destruction?" asked Sophia.

"I don't know. Maybe I did. They are gone, are they?" Demi, still shaken, yelled, "This is Uncle Theo's little joke again. He won't let us alone." They tried and tried to rest. At last the gentle thrumming of the drums calmed them and they slept.

An hour later, night-wandering Sophia and Cynique rose and walked silently into the village. Eulie patrolled from above. Sophia was still in her retracted mode, her normal night-aura quenched and shadowy, though she could see perfectly well. Cynique sniffed everywhere, gathering local information. Eulie's view was global. All was quiet. There were no lights in the houses, only the soft glowing fraxinella lights outside the houses, and the pyracanthine street lamps.

Yet, and yet, something was stirring. Sophia and Cynique froze. Eulie flew down and landed on Sophia's shoulder, turning her head in that remarkable manner of owls. "People are coming out of the houses. One at a time. Not all the houses, but some," Eulie reported.

Sophia whispered, "Keep looking. Keep on the watch. We might be in for trouble. Yes, now I can see the forms coming out of the houses." She peered more closely, "But they are not white."

Cynique reached up to her ear. "Oh," said Sophia, "Oh moon and stars above! This is so strange. These white ones are dressed in black. Even their faces are blackened." Sophia and Cynique moved silently to the edge of the square. They saw that the people, indeed in black, were assembling in the town square. They saw them dividing into groups of threes and fours, and walking about. When one group strolled casually near them, Sophia and Cynique took several quick steps to one side and were unobserved. The drumming began a low, intensive beat.

Sophia sent Cynique to shadow the group which had walked near them. She sent Eulie, in her camouflaged plumage, to trail after another group from above. They saw that the groups stopped milling about and all turned toward the side of the valley of the Phosphoros opposite where Demi and Sophia had bedded down. They fanned out throughout the length of the village and began to climb up toward the top of the vast range overlooking the Valley.

"What're they up to?" wondered Sophia. "It's as if they were on patrol," she thought. "Their clothing conceals them."

Hours passed. Cynique and Eulie reported periodically. And yes, the black-covered ones were walking silently along trails and peering about them, scouting the area. The drumming became increasingly louder in their ears.

Two hours before dawn there came a cry, and a great rushing of these black-robed ones toward the entrance of the village where Demi and Sophia had appeared the day before. There was yelling, and an agonized scream, then silence. Sophia ran to find Demi, who had been wakened by the noise, and explained what they had observed. They went cautiously to see what had happened.

They edged up to the crowd and saw that some among the on-lookers had begun to remove their dark outer clothing. They saw flaming torches and heard rough laughter and the rumble of gleeful conversation. They could see that there was some sort of form on the ground, a heap of rags. The group soon began to disperse, again in twos and threes, some kicking the pile, some taking hard jabs at it with walking sticks as they left. They returned to their houses, from which they had come: no noise, no lights, no disturbance. When all those white half-dressed-in-black creatures were gone at last, the four, Eulie, Cynique, Demi and Sophia cautiously approached the heap of rags for a closer look. The drumming stopped.

"Look closely. What do you see?" In the dim pre-dawn, dark-piercing Sophia pulled back a cloth and found a body. It was not the body of a very big person, but nonetheless a person, a person endowed with arms and legs and feet and head and nose and eyes and teeth, and lightly bronzed skin. It was lifeless. It was a body which had been contemptuously left. It was clearly an insignificant bundle, a trifling matter to be dealt with in the morning, a few twigs blown about by a sneeze, a pile of dung dropped by a goat sullying the purity of the alabaster paving.

As Sophia bent low to examine the body, the golden ball slipped out of her pocket. She reclaimed it and recalled its inscription: "For the fairest," it read.

Necrology

"Something's not fair here," said Demi, looking at the poor, shriveled body.

"That's true," said Sophia in her infinite wisdom, "though something else has just occurred to me. Think about where we are. I'm wondering if in this case we are intended to be thinking of another kind of *fair*: the *fair* of light, of whiteness, of brightness. 'For the fairest'. Who is the fairest?"

"Perhaps you're right, Sophia. But how could we possibly find someone here who would be the fairest? Fairest? Brightest? Whitest? Lightest colored? They all seem to be cut from the same cloth. Some are young. Some are old. Is there any one of them who is fairer, lighter in color, than any other? I'm inclined to think not. This is Uncle Theo's doing. That cursed man! That cursed ball! He has tricked us again."

And then, since they were tired from the long night and from the thousand questions they had about what they had seen, they returned to their camp exhausted, and slept.

But hardly, it seemed, had they fallen asleep when they heard a strong voice calling, "Weary travelers! Weary visitors! Wake up! I have brought food."

Demi and Sophia stirred and saw the village Presbyter standing before them. He carried bowls of snowy bread, and winter-colored bananas, and steaming ears of cloud corn, all of which he placed before them. Demi and Sophia thanked him, and, though they would not have thought so, nor would they have admitted it, they were hungry. When the Presbyter left, they ate the food and then reviewed the night's events, which, as ones well acquainted with mysteries, they easily categorized as dark doings.

They left their resting spot and walked into the village square. From a distance they could see where the body had been, but it was gone. In that place were three Phosphoros, forlornly sweeping and scrubbing the stones. Demi and Sophia walked over to see what was happening. When they innocently asked why the cleaning was going on in this particular spot, they were told, "We don't know. We were rousted from our warm beds and ordered to clean a dirty spot here, so here we are. We don't like filth on our whiteness, now do we?"

Demi and Sophia returned to their camping spot and waited. A single hoot from Eulie called them. Eulie landed on Sophia's shoulder and reported into her ear. Just before daylight, about the time that Sophia and Demi were trying to get to sleep, two of the Phosphoros had come with a stretcher and perfunctorily carried off the body. Cynique and Eulie followed the stretcher bearers as they walked for an hour and a half deep into the forest. They stopped at a vast sinkhole, into which the stretcher-bearers heedlessly dumped the body. After they left, Eulie and Cynique peered into the pit, where they saw the remains of other bodies, some skeletal, some still with the ragged remnants of their clothing wound about them.

Demi, normally sophisticated, unruffable, yelled, "Now we're really onto something. How can this happen? What's this all about? Let's go to the Archon's and find out. Let's demand some answers."

They walked across the length of the square, passing white ones running errands, some with children in hand, some carrying market baskets, some raising the shutters of their shops.

As they strode, Sophia and Demi grew in stature. A bass drum beat a heavy beat. They marched to it with their shoulders fully back and their heads high, the essence of authority. They became aristocratic, the antithesis of weariness.

This new appearance of Demi and Sophia caused a stir among the Phosphoros, who trailed timidly behind them. The appearance of Cynique walking beside Sophia and of Eulie swooping and swirling overhead particularly frightened the crowd, yet they followed.

Demi and Sophia were not standing nearly as tall and forceful looking as they had the day they grimly swooped down the center aisle in the Parliament of Judges building. They were what they were, sufficient for the moment. At length they reached the Archonery. With one final BAM from the drum.

Demi picked up a decorative white-washed stone and pounded on the door. "Come out!" she said. The Presbyter, out of breath, appeared from behind and tried to hush them.

"The Archon never appears before noon," he said. "It is his custom. It is the custom of the village."

Demi pounded again, and said formally, "I care nothing for such customs. Bring out the Archon or I'll send in this dog." Cynique's mouth curled.

The Presbyter disappeared behind the house and in a few moments, opened the front door. "The Archon will see you shortly," he announced, with uncertain dignity.

"I will wait exactly five minutes and then we will enter the house," Demi answered.

In a moment the Archon appeared in the doorway, leaning heavily on the Presbyter's shoulder. He stood for a moment peering at Demi and Sophia. His hands shook. His hair was in disarray. A white cloak barely hung over his left shoulder. "What is it you wish, weary travelers?" he whispered.

"You know full well," Sophia said. "We want to know the meaning of last night's events. Someone was killed on the square during the night, and the body was shamefully thrown into a common pit. We demand to know the reason for it." A murmur swept through the crowd.

"What is this?" said someone from the crowd. "What's this stranger talking about?" said others. The Archon turned to the Presbyter, who waved his hand, and the crowd dispersed.

The Archon looked at Sophia and Demi and glanced nervously at Cynique, then said, "What happens here is of no concern to you. I declare to you that you are not welcome in this village. Leave now." He turned abruptly and took a step into the building.

At this, Demi and Sophia shouted and pulled themselves up to an even greater extent. The Archon and the Presbyter fell back. Demi said, "Let us be clear that it is we who command here. We will come inside this building and you will explain what this life-taking is all about."

The Archon trembled at the sight of the two. He and the Presbyter meekly turned and entered the house, followed by Sophia and Demi. Cynique stayed at the entrance, on guard.

They found themselves in a short hallway. The Presbyter closed the outside door leaving Demi and Sophia at a disadvantage, unable to see because of the glare their eyes had been used to. They groped to find a wall, to find anything to orient them. Even night-loving Sophia was momentarily disoriented. The Presbyter opened another door and ushered them into a large, dark room in which two small candles were burning. When their eyes adjusted, they saw the Archon sitting on an immense throne. In his hand was a short white leafy branch.

He stood up, precipitously, and said, "Now what? You are not wanted here."

"Sit down!" said Demi. "You! Sit! I am in charge here. Now. Explain to me the killing of that person early this morning."

"It is nothing I can discuss, especially with you barbarians."

In the darkness Sophia began to glow, her whole person exuding light. The Archon and the Presbyter shrank back. Never had they seen such power. The light grew. The blackness disappeared. Demi and Sophia began to look around.

"Look!" said Sophia. Along one wall there hung a long row of black hooded cloaks. Nearby, in a corner of the room, leaned bundles of staffs. Over the cloaks and the staffs was posted a drawing of a creature similar to the one who lay dead that morning.

"What is the meaning of this?" asked Sophia. "Speak up. Look at all this. You proclaimed yourselves a people of peace, a people living in a utopia. What is the meaning of this?"

The Archon sat staring at Sophia, immobile.

"Do not be afraid to speak. But do not fail to speak. Or else you will become acquainted with the powers which stand before you."

At last he spoke. "What do you want to know? Who are you?"

Demi said, "We want an explanation of your behavior in killing someone and, now that we are here, we demand to know exactly why those black costumes and those heavy walking sticks are here. We demand to know the truth about you and this village. Come now, speak up."

"Tell me who you are," said the Archon.

"It is of no consequence to you," said Sophia.

"You want to know who I am, but you will not tell me who you are."

"Correct. As you can see, we are in command here," said Demi. "Begin speaking before we become angry. You do not want to feel our wrath."

"I will begin," he said, his shoulders sagging. "We are a simple people, and we live simple lives and we believe in purity and goodness in all and for all, but we live here in this valley under the threat of enemies who wish us evil. They wish to destroy us and our way of life because they can not abide our purity and joy."

"And so you kill those who come your way? Are your people ever in danger? Is anyone ever hurt or lost? Are they ever killed?" asked Demi. "I repeat: are any of your people killed? I want the truth."

The Archon said, "No, no, they are not. We have excellent defenses in place, you see."

"What I see," said Demi, "is that you are hypocrites. Terrible, ruthless hypocrites. You masquerade as peace-loving innocent people who worship the Sun and purity, and yet you kill.

"Tell, me, Master Archon," she continued, "What are those things in the corner? No, not the sticks and cloaks, but those things in the other corner?" Demi had seen two green bowls and a dark blue basket. "Bring them to me." She paused as she looked at them. "These are not yours because everything you produce is white. So, what are these things and where did they come from?"

She held in her hand a gracefully burnished thin-sided emerald-green bowl. A simple pot with no obvious use, except that it was made for the love of making it. She set it gently down on the Archon's table and picked up the blue basket. It was ingeniously woven, with red flower patterns embedded in the very weave itself, clearly evident that it was woven with blue grasses.

"Where did these come from?" demanded Sophia. The Archon hesitated, and the Presbyter answered.

"Sometimes in the mornings we find them in the square, several of them grouped together." He paused. "We destroy them, of course, because we know they are from them. Those people. Those dark people. The evil ones."

"If I understand, this means that these *dark* people have been able to penetrate your defenses at will and they have often left these beautiful items for you in plain sight on the square," said Sophia. She loomed over the two pale creatures. "And what do you presume that leaving these items means? Have you ever considered it?"

The Archon spoke, drawing himself up tall. "We presume it to be danger when we find them. They invade our sacred space secretly. They mean to overwhelm us. They are taunting us."

"O Ignorant One, is it possible that they've left you sweet and pleasant gifts? Exquisite gifts from their hearts? Consider the fineness of this bowl. Look at the intricacy, the skill it took to weave this basket. I believe it might even hold water, so tightly has it been woven. Why would you be taunted with such marvels by enemies?" asked Sophia. "Please do me a favor. Consider what other message might be arrived at from these items left in the very center of your village square."

The Archon thought. "There is no other message to be derived from these evil items. I shall have these vessels that you have been fondling destroyed before the Sun is high."

"Oh," said Sophia, "what hypocrites you are. How you blaspheme life itself. Look at you. Here you are living in this darkened place, where you are happily shielded from the blinding light and the heat of the day. You and your people are living lies. What great pretenders you are.

"Is it possible that these tan-skinned people whom you so freely murder are constantly seeking to find you and to be a part of your lives? Think! Think! They appear to be determined, though you kill them. They offer you gifts after easily entering the village. After they have been abroad on the village green.

Have they disturbed the peace or vandalized your village? Do they not come in peace?"

The Archon closed his eyes. He imperiously waved them away. He opened the door and stood to one side, as if to wave Demi and Sophia out. But they stood fast. He closed the door.

"Bring me a staff," the Archon said to the Presbyter, "and take one yourself. These creatures are leaving." Taking a staff he placed the Presbyter alongside him, and began to lift the staff up and down making a series of three thumps. The Presbyter joined him. Thump, thump, THUMP. Thump, thump, THUMP. Thump, thump, THUMP. The tempo of the thumping gradually increased. Thump, thump, THUMP.

Demi and Sophia watched silently. From the Archon came a murmuring. Words fell on Demi and Sophia, which at first they could not understand, words that accompanied the thump-thump-THUMP. Only slowly did the incantations of the Archon's litany seep into their consciousness.

The Archon's litany: "Go you forth, Harpies, leave this place, Scylla. Go away Charybdis, be gone, iconoclasts. Depart from our village, O Hysterics, fly from us, you exotics. Have no more to do with us, O Gynecological misfits. Run away you nomads. Interfere with us never again, you deceiving diabolics. Vanish, you misanthropes."

Louder and louder came the thumping. Louder and louder sounded the chanting. Sophia and Demi stared at the Archon. Their hands covered their ears. They shut their eyes. The thumping continued. The voice became stronger.

A movement of air caused Demi and Sophia to open their eyes. They saw that a dozen hooded forms clad in black robes and holding staffs surrounded them. The staffs were aimed at Demi and Sophia, and the black-robed forms gestured menacingly at them.

The staff-men circled. They feinted blows at the two. Then they joined in the thump, thump, thumping on the floor with their staffs.

The creatures in black hummed tunelessly as the Archon continued his monotonous song.

Demi and Sophia looked at each other and began to scream. It was a scream which grew higher and higher in brute force, overwhelming the thump, thump, thump until, at its climax, their howling burst into the very being of Archon and his acolytes, leaving them, Archon, Presbyter and the black-clad ones lying on the floor moaning, their hands jammed against their ears.

Looking down on their inert forms, Sophia and Demi imperiously said as one. "Arise. Get on your feet and hear us." The Presbyter reached over and helped the Archon stand. All the others, staggering from the screaming blast, also stood.

Demi spoke. "There is much to say here, O Archon of Archons. May I congratulate you on your poetic grasp, on the fluid musicality of your vocabulary? What symphonies! What rhapsodies we found ourselves in as you sang. What keenly orchestrated condemnations. You surely have given us much to think about.

"In your chanting, O Archon, you categorize us in many ways. You accuse us in many ways. Yet, at heart you charge us with interfering with your life." She paused.

"Well, we will acknowledge that soon after we entered Phosphoro we became suspicious. We did so without knowing the full extent of your story. Thanks to you we now understand it more fully."

The Archon bowed in acknowledgement.

"But," Sophia continued, "We believe no less that you are wrong to condemn those you call the Dark Ones. You are wrong to live pretending you are pure and innocent. You are wrong to isolate yourselves and condemn others who differ from you.

"Fine words," said the Archon. "Fine words. But you do not know what you are saying or who we are dealing with. You do not know how evil the Dark Ones are."

"Then let us find out," said Sophia. "Let's explore, let's find out. It's something we weary travelers love to do. Come, let's explore, and I will take some of your people with me."

"That can never be. No one will accompany you. They are all too afraid," said the Archon.

"Send these people away," said Demi pointing at the hooded ones. The Archon pointed and waved his hand and the black robes were removed, the staffs set once again in their corner. The white ones slipped out the back door of the Archonery and into the wince-making sunshine.

"I will take this Presbyter," said Sophia, "and the two guards who met us at the entrance to the village."

The Presbyter's wide eyes appealed to the Archon, then he slipped behind him.

Sophia said, "He will go with us. Tell him."

The Archon turned and gave the Presbyter a gentle shove. "Yes, it is as you wish. Presbyter, inform the two guards." He added, looking directly at Demi and Sophia, "I warn you. You two do not know what it is that you do."

Demi said, "They are to leave their weapons here. We go in peace. We go tonight."

That evening, after the villagers bid farewell to the Sun, after a meal, after the fraxinella and pyracantha bushes had been lighted, after the village quieted for the night, Demi and Sophia were once again resting on the soft porphyrial pods under the spreading diasporal bush.

As soon as it was dark, Sophia sent Eulie and Cynique on a scouting expedition. With Eulie towering overhead, Cynique ran toward the ridge opposite Sophia and Demi, and both disappeared from view.

As she watched them, Demi said sadly, "I keep wondering about Cora. Is she safe? We simply must find Uncle Theo. We must get to Tophat."

Sophia, trying to see Eulie, replied, "Perhaps this is the way we are meant to go in our search. Maybe Uncle Theo is over there."

Eulie returned long before Cynique. He whispered into Sophia's ear. Sophia said to Demi, "He flew to the top of that ridge opposite and reports that on the other side all is blackness. Absolute darkness. He flew down as far as he dared over the edge, but was unable to see anything at all."

Sophia whispered that she wondered if Eulie weren't aging a bit.

"I'm confident that when we get there we'll find no obstruction."

Cynique returned. Demi learned from the black dog that the way was clear and that there was no one abroad. But Cynique admitted that he had not reached the top.

"It's time to depart. Sophia, gather those three white ones." Soon the troop was on its way: the Presbyter, an unarmed spearman, a mirror-less mirrorman, an owl, a dog, a fearless mother and her moon-besotted daughter.

A snare drum rolled gently.

Eros

After the awkward dinner party, Cora heard nothing from Tophat DeVille. Her spies told her that he had immediately left on a long journey. Her friends told her she had been too forward, to which she replied that she had no idea that she was in dangerous territory when she had asked Tophat if he knew Demi and Sophia. She wondered what had made those names pop into her mind, for they were a faded memory. She went about her business, reading and learning and passionately following where paths of inquiry led her. Tophat was forgotten.

One day – weeks later – Rhoda appeared carrying an envelope for her. Inside, she found a note from Tophat inquiring about her health and thanking her, at long last, for the fine dinner. Then he asked whether she would be interested in seeing the greenhouses where the daffodil experiments were carried out.

Cora conferred with Xantippe saying, "I'd really like to see the experiments." But Xantippe urged her to wait a week before replying, so as not to seem too eager.

Reluctantly, because of her interest in flowers, Cora allowed the week to pass, though she did not understand precisely why. At last she wrote him and, still guided by Xantippe, her response was cautious. She supposed she could find time (she was sorry for the delay in responding, but she had been quite busy), and she also supposed that such a botanical venture was of some passing interest to her. She would accept the invitation, though she could spare only an hour or so because of the press of her studies – perhaps next week.

A time was agreed to, and late one morning Tophat DeVille came for her in his carriage and they went to the greenhouses. Cora was intrigued by technicians' explanations of their experiments, and of their goals, and the intricacy of their note keeping. She loved seeing the pots of flowers in various stages of development. Sian and Chloris came in from working with the daffodils, but they and Cora pretended they did not know each other. Tophat knew otherwise and said nothing.

Shortly, she said she needed to go home again because of work she didn't dare leave for long. Tophat agreed, only if she would have lunch with him first. She said yes and they dined together at his home, surrounded by servants. Rhoda was there serving fresh baked goods, but Cora and Rhoda pretended they did not know each other. Tophat knew otherwise and said nothing.

Two days later Tophat knocked at the door of Cora's apartment, offering to give her a tour around The Necropolis in his carriage. She said, "I can go tomorrow afternoon at two."

That tour was the first of many. After that initial drive through the immense fields of daffodils, of asphodels, of jonquils, and of narcissus, he took her from time to time to see new monuments, interesting new cenotaphs, and a recently completed columbarium decorated with impish doves. Once they went to see a sweet little crypt that some exotic had ordered.

Sometimes he stopped off at her apartment with foods he had found on his travels. Cora smiled.

Just as many times he just popped in unannounced with no invitation in hand. She would stand at the door with an exasperated look on her face, her hands on her hips, and shake her finger "No, no, no," at him, and then tell him she was studying or too busy and that she could not be interrupted just then. "Please go away," she would say, and he went.

Yet, Cora was mixed in her thoughts. She enjoyed the rides in the carriage and the occasional meals. Then there were the gifts he gave her. Pearls. Often pearls from the sea. Emeralds. Usually from high in the mountains. Flowers. From remote spots, with droll faces, even though in a few hours they fell limp. Who would go so far as to bring a flower from so far to please her, knowing it would soon be gone?

One day when he came for a ride through The Necropolis, she became aware of the crowds. Why hadn't she noticed them before? Cora asked about them and began to learn about the business side of The Necropolis. There were those who came for burial below in the dank catacombs and those who took advantage of burial in the beautiful grounds with their whimsical statues and monuments.

"This is an interesting business, Tophat," she said.

"Yes, indeed. It keeps many of us busy, and it's profitable, if I may say so. I do a lot of traveling because of it. Always searching for ideas which will enhance the property." He noticed that she was sitting closer to him, and that, even better, she had slipped her arm through his. He perked up considerably.

When he took her home, she invited him to come into the apartment for a cup of tea. He happened to glance at the paintings. The little girls, the sailors, the watchmen, the pearly sphinx of the paintings, all of them, had turned and were watching him.

She brought him tea, which they sipped slowly. They sat in silence and she looked at him for a long time. When they finished their tea Cora said, "I must get back to work. Thank you for the nice time. Goodbye." As Tophat went out the door, Cora gave him a kiss on the cheek, gave him a little shove, and closed the door firmly. The painting people returned to their preoccupations.

The next time he came in, he stayed for the night.

Cora and Tophat became partners in The Necropolis enterprise. Tophat was acutely aware of her intelligence and of the asset it was. In addition, Cora's studies, she discovered, led her to an interest in architecture, which in turn led her to design and oversee the construction of a reception center for The Necropolis, a building Tophat had wanted for some time.

Tophat DeVille was loyal to Cora as a partner and was a lover, though it hardly meant that he became a different person. Cora was aware that his interest in his collection of females had not flagged, nor could she realistically expect otherwise. There were two occasions, however, when she was able to take action. In the first instance, she caught him with a recently arrived victim flagrantly driving through the daffodils in The Necropolis. In collaboration with her friends, Rhoda and Xantippe, she had this one quietly removed to work in poplar groves beyond The Necropolis.

Another young victim of Tophat's hobby was discovered by Cora in Tophat's apartment and stealthily removed. This second poor child found herself assigned to toil in the mint groves.

Both victims became less attractive to Tophat with the passage of time, as their hands showed the signs of hard work and their faces wrinkled from the sun.

Nor was Cora's loyalty to Tophat immune to other influences. One day, while she was working in the reception center, a truly boyish young man approached her to make arrangements, in advance, for the burial of an aged aunt, who appeared to be making a career out of being near death. Cora looked at his face and felt a never-known shiver thrill through her; certainly never, ever with Tophat DeVille. Certainly never. She felt dizzy. "A god!" she thought. "Good Lord in heaven. What a beautiful young man. He is staring at me, too. See how his mouth has dropped open. And he is smiling. Both at once. How can he do that? What is this?"

Cora, usually cool and objective in her work with mourners, stammered, "I think we should confer about your aunt in a conference room. Follow me." In the room her adonic young man told her his name and what he needed (the aunt, of course). They fell into each other's arms. Cora went to the door and locked it, and pulled the curtains, and that was that.

When at last they talked, he said, "I've realized something, Cora. I'm fortunate to have many truly ancient relatives. I'll be coming frequently."

She said, "And my professional assessment of your situation is that it's urgent that you always come and confer with me ahead of time, well before any deaths." To her joy, her handsome friend visited her frequently. Life was complete for Cora.

But it did not last. There came a time when she realized he had not appeared for two weeks. That was rare. More time passed. Cora searched within herself for reasons. Didn't he care for her anymore? Was there something she'd said which offended him? Had something happened to him?

Then Xantippe came one day with news. Her beautiful boy was dead, killed by a wild animal while he was hunting. Cora grieved at the thought of his death and at the manner of his dying. She wept. She sobbed. She would not be consoled, though surrounded by friends who mourned with her. Chloris planted a garden of anemones in his memory.

At last Cora recovered. She was soon able to hold her head high. When she was ready, she summoned Tophat, and told him everything, and Tophat comforted her. But Cora never completely forgot her young man, and the excitement of their love. Through the passing years occasionally something would occur – a word, an incident, a similarity of someone's eyes or cut of hair – that reminded her of her beautiful boyish boy. Then, even if for a moment, her passion welled up. Cora never completely forgot him.

Demos

Demi and Sophia and the others climbed the ridge, following the series of long switchbacks on their way to discover what there was to know about the little bronze ones. When they were a little more than half way up, they came to a clearing where they could look back down on the village of the Phosphoros. A half moon spilled light on the quiet town. The pale glow of the burning bushes and the soft streetlights defined the houses and the shops and the streets. "What a sweet and lovely sight," sighed Sophia. "Yet," she yelled, "Liars! Liars! Terrible creatures!" The drum roll softened.

They continued their climb and at last reached the crest and looked over it, but there was nothing to see. Ahead lay Nothing. Absolutely Nothing. It was as Eulie had said. The Presbyter and the soldiers shuddered and turned their backs on the dark and comforted themselves by peering down at the glow from the distant refuge.

Sophia took a few steps down the trail into the blackness, confident that she, with her penetrating vision could conquer the gloom. But it was no good. Her vision was swallowed as surely as a tossed stone plummets into the ocean. She stepped back quickly.

Cynique dared take a few steps down the trail but was swallowed up, too. He disappeared into the black as surely as a rock sinks into the sea. He turned and, thanks to his sense of smell, found his way back.

Demi called out, "Hello!" but her voice was swallowed into nothing as surely as a pebble disappears into the deep.

Seeing it, the Presbyter and the two soldiers whimpered. The mirror-soldier, he of the senseless weapon, said "Please! Let's go back. Please! Not even the moon or our dear Sun, could lighten this darkness, no matter how we beseech them."

Demi, taking it all in, trembled at the fearsome black. Though unnerved by their failed attempts, she kept her disquiet to herself. Summoning up her public best, she said at last, "Well, let's sit down here quietly and wait to see what will happen. Just sit down," she said, "but careful where you sit, and be quiet." They sat, amazed at the nothingness before them.

Sophia whispered, "Is this another cleverness of Uncle Theo?"

None of them could recollect later how long they sat saying nothing, peering intently at nothing, hearing nothing. All they remembered later was that after a time there came a high voice from not so far away saying "Welcome weary strangers!" followed by a loud shushing. If Demi and the others gasped, if they could have looked at each other in wonder, they would have.

There immediately followed a gleeful laugh as of a child, and more shushing. Then there were more laughing voices here and there, and then even more, as if a dam had broken. Once the laughter started, it was as if it was infectious. Even the quick-to-shush must have given in to uncontrolled hilarity.

Demi and Sophia and the others were puzzled by what they were hearing, yet they began to have the impression that this laughter was not evil, but rather the laughter which comes from those who are happy about something and who hope that "something" never stops.

Sophia asked, "What is going on here? Why this laughter? Is there some sort of comedy going on here? Is this real? Is this Uncle Theo again?"

In a moment Demi answered, "It seems to me that everything is all right. This is no trick. This is happening."

A gong sounded, and with it the laughter died away. It was eerily still. The seven on the ridge crest, peering into absolute nothing, sat without moving, though Demi wondered why they did so. It was obvious that whoever was out there in the darkness knew perfectly well that there were seven of them sitting down and looking into the black, and that someone knew exactly who they were.

"I'm going to speak," Demi announced. What else was there to do?

She stood. "Hello," she called into the black. "Hello to you from the weary travelers."

At this there came a booming chorus, a choir as of thousands, "Hello to you, weary travelers."

Sophia thought *well, well* to herself, then added a loud "Hello." Eulie hooted and Cynique barked. "Hellos" came back. The white ones from Phosphoro froze.

Demi, emboldened, said, "We want to come to you but we can not see. Can you light the way?"

A voice responded, "What is the business you have with us, weary travelers?"

There was silence for a time while Demi considered what to say, and then she answered, "We want to meet you. We want to know you. We want to learn about you. We want to share ideas with you. We want to see if we can be of help to you."

Silence surrounded them again. Moments and minutes passed. The seven trembled. Then, a voice:

"Weary travelers."

"Yes, we hear you."

"Weary travelers, you may come to see us. You simply start walking down the path before you."

"But we can not see a path – any path. We are blind. We fear we may fall. We can not move."

"Ah, weary travelers. That is the condition. Begin to walk into what you do not know."

"Do you assure that it will be well?" called Sophia.

"Stand. Begin to walk. Trust. You will see."

Demi stood, resolved. "Come here, Cynique. Let us begin." Cynique pressed tightly against Demi's side. The tympani beat a marching step, the two stepped into the blackness, and were gone.

At this, the Presbyter and the two soldiers panicked and yelled "Oh, no! Oh, no! No! Not us!" Turning around, they started down the ridge toward the village. But Sophia, who had been concentrating entirely on Demi's step into the dark, became conscious – somehow – of the white ones' desperate shouts and whipped around in time to catch them in the act of desertion. She lunged toward them and falling forward, locked onto the foot of one of them, thwarting his escape.

The other two dove arrow-straight down the ridge toward the village of the Phosphoros. Caring nothing for the switchbacks, they stumbled and rolled straight down against bushes and roots and stones and trees, bloodying their paper-white skins and biting great hunks out of the insides of their cheeks, until many minutes later they were on the valley floor, where they lay, unable to rise, panting in the cool whiteness, happy to await the dawn and offering praises to the Sun that they had escaped ruin.

Sophia turned to see whose foot she had gripped in the confusing darkness. She had landed the Presbyter.

"You mewling, leukodermic, whiteskin! Sit until I tell you otherwise," she said, and ordered Eulie to stand in front of the

Presbyter, her claws unfurled, ready to spring. The white mouse froze.

Almost immediately the voice from the dark announced, "Come. Next. Commence." The tympani continued the beat.

Sophia stood and taking the Presbyter by the scruff of his neck, pushed him in front of her. He protested. He whined. But Sophia was adamant. Eulie perched on Sophia's shoulder, scooting himself as close to Sophia's neck as he could.

Sophia and the Presbyter stepped timidly into the inkiness, as Demi had done. With one arm clutching the Presbyter, Sophia bent her other arm before her for protection, as doubtless Demi had done. All sound was swallowed up. In the disorienting blackness, Sophia closed her eyes, enabling her to visualize what was happening to her step by step, as surely Demi had done.

She was aware of the Presbyter swaying heavily ahead of her, of his resisting her pushing, of her heart pulsing, of the rapid breaths she was drawing, of her body moving forward step by step, though she could not seem to feel her feet. She had no sense of time.

"Courageous traveler, open your eyes," came a voice. "It is light here."

Sophia opened her eyes slowly. At first she could barely discern the form of the Presbyter ahead of her, her grip still firmly on his shoulder. They continued walking.

"Courageous traveler, you do not need to assist any one." Sophia dropped her hold on the Presbyter. Her eyes gradually became accustomed to the light, and slowly she became aware that ahead of her were dozens, perhaps scores of figures like the sad one she and Demi had found dead in the Village of the Phosphoros. The drumbeat stopped.

Sophia became aware that all those figures were softly clapping their hands and laughing and smiling. Several of them walked slowly to meet them. Some took the Presbyter's hands and escorted him toward the others. Similarly, others gleefully took Sophia's hands. The clapping of those smiling figures intensified, and there in the center of those figures sat Demi.

"You weren't long," called Demi, "were you? Look around you. Isn't this a nice place?"

It took Sophia a moment or two to realize what she was seeing. There in warm yellow light were scores and scores of little tan creatures, draped in colorful cloaks. Indeed, these lively bronzed beings were precisely like the one she and Demi had seen lying dead in the village below just that morning, its blood sullying the purity of the white pavement.

Yet, there they were, clapping their hands and smiling and beckoning, beckoning to her, smiling welcomes to her. Demi sat smiling, surrounded by the little beings. It surprised Sophia that she found pleasure in the gentle touch of their hands as they guided her to Demi.

The Presbyter, once he too was able to focus on the scene around him, shuddered. Waves of iciness, of dread, of terror, passed over him again and again, for he recognized in these little creatures their brothers whom he had helped destroy.

He pictured himself, brutal staff in hand, crashing it down on the rib cage of a little one, now on the groin, now on the neck and the face, breaking its nose, crushing its teeth, and exulting in his work.

And here he was in the midst of these creatures, shivering in fear.

Yet, there they were, smiling at him and crowding around him, taking his hands and leading him. Some shouted, "Welcome Grand Presbyter! Welcome. We're glad you have come here. Welcome! Welcome!"

Singing began. Bodies began to sway gently. "Welcome, welcome" thrummed as an underlying chorus.

Their journey through the dark had led Sophia, Demi, the Presbyter, Eulie, and Cynique to the entrance of a vast cavern filled with the little creatures.

Soft light filled the space and happy shouts echoed from chamber to chamber. They could see the openings into other rooms, into rooms without end.

At last one of the creatures, somewhat taller than the others, stood and signaled for quiet. He smiled at them. He reached out and softly caressed Cynique and Eulie, then spoke. "Welcome to the home of the Demos, the People. How honored we are by your presence, by your willingness to make this odyssey through the blackness into the light of our home. You are our honored guests. And – please – let me introduce myself. I am called the Adelphos here. I am the appointed leader of the Demos."

Demi spoke, "O Adelphos, Brother, we are honored to be here, but I must tell you that I am puzzled. You called us 'weary travelers' when we were preparing for the trial of the dark, and you called this one 'Presbyter.' How can that be? How did you know?"

The Adelphos smiled, and soft laughter rippled through the Demos. "Yes, we did. Indeed. But you see it's not magic. We know about you and your visit to Phosphoro. Oh, and we know the Phosphoros people very well. We know the Archon and the Presbyter very, very well." The Presbyter raised his head sharply. His mouth dropped open and he stared at the Adelphos. Fear for the future coursed through him.

The leader continued, "Yes, we know everything that happens in the village below. In the evening when the Sun goes down, we descend to the village. We stand near the windows and listen to the conversations. We quietly make our way around the village. We often dress in white and blend in with the crowd in their activities. Two of us were even in the house of the Archon when that debate raged early today.

"Our two wielded staffs and pounded them fearfully. We saw how you won and also learned that you would climb the ridge tonight, so we prepared for you. We regret that the two soldiers were so cowardly. We would have gladly greeted them."

"This is not possible," said the Presbyter. "Surely it can not be true. We have our eyes and ears everywhere in the village. You cannot have been in the Archon's Center. We would have seen you."

"Would you like me to repeat exactly what happened and what words were spoken? I can tell you precisely. First, Demi and Sophia pounded at the door, furious because of the slaying of one of our brother Demos, though they did not know who or what he was. They were angry at the murder. Then they entered the Archon's house."

"Enough! You don't have to say more. I believe you."

The leader said, "That is indeed enough for now. Come. It's time to rest. Tomorrow we'll show you more of the Demos' home and you will come to know us."

He led them through a tunnel where they had to bow their heads a little, and then into a soft blue room. "Here you will rest for the night. Food is on its way."

They feasted on panegyric bread and a fine symmetric soup. They pulled downy stalactite comforters over themselves and slept.

In the morning the Adelphos appointed several of the Demos to show them around their home. They found valleys and lakes and streams and windy places. They entered rooms that were mined for the minerals, which were used to create the dyes for their colorful clothing and to make paints for general use.

They passed grottos where families lived and crystal caves where many Demos worked carving intricate vessels. Demi, Sophia, and the Presbyter were stunned by the color everywhere. Many rooms shone with yellows and blues. Other areas featured reds and pinks and complimentary greens.

The force of the color assailed the Presbyter, as if he were tasting sweetness for the first time. Gradually his eyes, his consciousness, adjusted to the colors that he was incapable of describing. Once, long ago he had seen colors, but only in small quantities. The Archon showed him a small book, kept in a secret spot, in which brilliant feathers were preserved. The book was marked "Evil". He later recalled them as the merest introduction to color.

Perhaps most surprising of all, no matter how much deeper they went into the mountain, it was nearly sunny everywhere.

When he became aware of the light, the Presbyter asked, "How can there be light in here so far from the entrance?"

"I have been wondering about that for some time," said Sophia.

As they looked about, the Adelphos appeared. "We are amazed at the brilliance of the light," said Sophia.

"You no doubt are," said the Adelphos. "Can you guess?" he asked Sophia. She looked thoughtful.

"Give me a moment. Light is at my soul and I enjoy puzzling things out. They don't remain puzzles for very long." She walked about. She touched a wall. She looked at the ceiling. She looked down on a labyrinth of pathways below them. She looked back as far as she could in the direction from which they had come.

"Here is how you provide light," she said at last. "You have used photosynthesis and bioluminescence to capture the daylight outside the cavern, and you send it throughout the inside. During the evening hours, you multiply the phosphorescence of the rock many times over to provide light. At night the light is naturally softer. I assume this is correct."

"Exactly," said the Adelphos. "There is little you don't know."

"I know," said Sophia.

They walked on and the Adelphos said, "Here's something I want you to see. You will enjoy this."

They came upon a vast room, a cathedral of a room. All at once a crowd of Demos, which had gradually been growing behind the visitors, began gleefully shouting and rushed past the Adelphos and the others, nearly knocking them down in their eagerness to get into the room. "As you can see," said the Adelphos, "this is our gymnasium. We are like little children in there."

The vast room was filled with blocks and towers and swing ropes and running space. The blocks were flexible so that the Demos could jump on them and bounce over another block, or bounce from one block to another. Many climbed the towers and jumped off trapezoid style, landing on a bouncing block, doing isosceles flips as they dropped. Their physical prowess amazed the on-lookers. Cynique joined the fun, leaping from one block to another, sometimes spinning like a rhombus. Little Demos jumped on him and tried to hold on, but always spilled off, causing enormous laughter, time after time. Eulie, a born acrobat, flew up and around and swooped up and down and looped the loops. Demos kids tried to catch him as he flew by.

Some of the older Demos engaged in calisthenics off to one side, avoiding the enthusiastic leaping and bounding of the younger ones.

The Presbyter, Demi, Sophia, and the Adelphos stood watching the antics from a safe distance. After a few moments, Demi, smiling, turned to see how the Presbyter was enjoying the show, but he was gone.

Astonished, she immediately turned to her right to see if he had somehow moved to where the others stood, but he was not there. Anxiously, she looked behind her. There she found him, sitting on a small plinth, hands folded in his lap, his eyes fixed on the ground. For some minutes Demi watched him. He kept staring at the ground, until, perhaps because of a shout or a sudden movement from the gymnasium, he raised his head, and peered around. He stood, unsteadily, still looking around, as if orienting himself. Then he threw his shoulders back and looked at the Adelphos. He stepped over to him, saying, "Brother Adelphos, I must speak with you. It is urgent."

"Of course," said the Adelphos. "But, let's move away from here." They headed back down the corridor from the gymnasium." Demi touched Sophia's arm.

"Come. Let's follow them. This may be important."

The men stepped into a small grotto. Sophia and Demi were right behind and stood near. The Presbyter paid no attention to them.

"My Brother Adelphos, I must return to my village and I must return right now."

"How disappointing, Friend Presbyter. I was in hopes that you would stay two or three more days so that you would really be able to know us well."

"That is thoughtful, but for now I've learned enough, and I can assure you that I will be back. What have I learned? I've been able to contrast your way of life with ours. Our way, as far as I can tell, is deficient."

"Yes, but what have you truly learned?" asked the Adelphos.

"Well, I have observed that in contrast to you Demos, we Phosphoros are a passive people. We really do nothing. We just 'are'. Our routines never vary and we take pride in that. But, you… you are creative, inventive people. You stimulate one another and enjoy your discoveries. Our scientists are devoted, in one sense, to destruction. They remove color so that all is white.

"But here I notice that you revel in color. It is all around. Look at those youngsters in the gymnasium. See the many colors they wear? Some wear many colors. The apparatuses they play on are green and blue. The very walls of the Gymnasium are brilliant with yellows and reds.

"I've concluded that color is the key to your society. It stimulates creativity, is energizing, and has a kaleidoscopic effect. Brother Adelphos, I want to return to my people, the Phosphoros, and introduce them to a new way of being, to encourage them to cast off the stultifying effect of white and white only. Oh, believe me, I'll be back, and I'll be bringing others with me, if you will permit it."

"Of course, of course you may. They'll be welcome."

"And, Brother Adelphos, I'd like several of the Demos to accompany me when I leave. They'd be with me for only a few hours, and then they would be able to return here. They'll be safe, I promise you. No harm will come to them."

"It is well," said the Adelphos. "Of course you can leave. I give permission for you to go. I look forward to hearing how this experiment goes, and I wish you well in it. Depart in peace."

"Thank you," said the Presbyter. Then, after a moment he added, "What did you mean by saying that you give me 'permission to leave?' Do I need permission?"

"Oh, my friend, I had hoped," replied the Adelphos, "that you'd stay here several days more, so that you'd come to know us. To be practical about it, you need permission because you'd never be able to find your way out. In a way you are unintentionally detained. For more than one reason you need permission."

"But," said the Presbyter, "I do feel I know you. I don't feel detained. I've observed your hospitality; I've eaten your food. We've walked through the caves and grottos and crossed rivers and streams. I've noted your use of color, and the remarkable way you use the spaces here, and the playfulness of the people here."

"And," said the Adelphos, "Am I to suppose those trifling observations fully describe us? They are true enough, but superficial. Hardly helpful. Let me ask: What do you know of the way we govern ourselves? Of the way we are organized? Of our economics? What do you know of our strategies when we are in danger? What do you know of the way we organize our families and our pedagogical methods? What of the way we resolve conflict (for even among us we do not always agree)? What do we do in the event of catastrophes? What of our knowledge of the cosmos? How do you think we feed ourselves? How do we feed our minds?"

The Presbyter gazed at his shoes for a long time. At last he said, "You're right," looking the Adelphos in the eye. "I admit I know nothing about you." He paused. "But I want to learn about you. I will come back. Many times. And I'll bring the wisest of our people with me that we may learn. We have much to learn. But right now I must go down to the village and assure them all is well, and to tell them of my experience with you and stir up in them a vision for a better way. I must go down before they become excited and send out search parties in hopes of finding any Demos, and possibly kill them."

"You may go."

"But Sir, you didn't answer a question I asked earlier. Will you allow some of the Demos to go with me? Few of our people have seen your people, and it is essential that they do. I assure you that all will be well. They'll return tonight after dark."

Brother Adelphos thought for a long time. He looked back at the gymnasium. He looked at his people passing up and down the corridors. He nodded. "Yes. I'll send some of our people with you. I'll trust you, and yet I must warn you that we can make life difficult if anything amiss happens."

"I understand," said the Presbyter. "But don't forget that Sophia and Demi will be there with us. They'll be on guard. And they are powerful."

"That's certainly true," said the Adelphos. "Now, then, let us leave." Off they went: Sophia and Demi and Brother Adelphos and the Presbyter. They followed Cynique and Eulie, who knew the way.

At last they reached the entrance to the cavern. Brother Adelphos left them briefly and returned with five young Demos. "They will accompany you."

"They're familiar with your village below. They've been there many times. One of them was in the house of the Archon two days ago during the confrontation with Demi and Sophia. They also know about the charnel pit where our brothers' bodies lie."

"It is well," said the Presbyter. "But let's leave. There's only an hour until the farewell to the Sun, and I want to be there when it is over. The whole village will be there to see us."

The Adelphos was carrying a small bundle of cloth, which he handed the Presbyter. "Here, open this when you arrive at the village."

"Thank you," said the Presbyter, surprised by the gift. He handed it to one of the Demos to carry.

They walked the path from the mouth of the cavern to the crest of the ridge. The Presbyter led the way, his face a mixture of smiles and frowns.

Behind him followed Demi and Sophia. Cynique brushed against Sophia. Eulie whirled exultantly above. The five Demos, dressed in greenish blues, reddish pinks, and blinding yellows, came last.

The Sun was nearing its setting as they prepared to descend. Sophia sent Eulie flying down to see what he could see and report back. Eulie soon returned with news that the village was reeling because of the disappearance of the Presbyter, and upset by the terrifying tales told by the two soldiers who had deserted the others on the ridge the night before. But even so, they were beginning to say their farewells to the Sun.

Just before they started down, the Presbyter looked back toward the cavern. But there was nothing, absolutely nothing. He yelled. He pointed. Sophia and Demi looked back and gasped. There was nothing to see. Where there had been a mountain with a cavernous opening just below, there was only darkening sky. They carefully walked a few feet back in the direction from which they had come and found themselves on the sharp edge of a cliff. Massive boulders lay below. The cavern and the mountain had disappeared. They looked at the Demos. They, too, looked back, but they showed no concern. "Is this one of Theo's tricks?" asked Sophia.

"Maybe," said Demi. "Perhaps."

The descent went steadily. They walked quietly so that they would not attract attention below. Sophia sent Eulie on a scouting mission. She returned with word that the Phosphoros were gathering at the Farewell Hill.

The troupe reached the village area but stayed hidden behind the snowy trees. The Presbyter looked out. "They're all at the Hill," he said. "What do we do now?"

Demi said, uncharacteristically, "What do you think is the best plan?"

Speaking quietly, the Presbyter said, "Let's go stand together, in a row, so that the people see us when they come back. Let's do it now while they're saying their farewells." As the light faded, they moved into the village square, following the Presbyter's lead. He stopped about fifty yards from the Farewell Hill. "Let's stand in a row," he said quietly. "Demi, you and Sophia on this hand and you, my friends, on the other side," he said to the Demos.

It was only a moment or two before the Phosphoros turned around and began to walk quietly back into the village. Children started racing back, but tumbled to a stop at the strange sight: the Presbyter, their own beloved pure-white Presbyter, flanked by those two strange women on one side and the colorfully dressed creatures on the other. The children shouted, "Look, everybody, look!" The older Phosphoros stopped moving. At first they whispered, then their voices raised to shouts of wonder. They pointed at the strange group before them. But the Presbyter gestured to them to come on ahead. "Come on. Come here," he commanded.

"Come on. Come on. We want you to see something wonderful." It was indeed something of wonder for the Phosphoros. They edged forward slowly. They paid no attention to the Presbyter or to Demi and Sophia. Their eyes fixed on the Demos, those little people who had not been seen by most of them before. Even as the light began to fade the Phosphoros easily saw the colors on the Demos. Colors! A phenomenon unknown to them. Colors! Look at the colors.

Colors had been spoken of abstractly, uncomprehendingly, in whispers at night between husbands and wives snuggled up in their beds. They had seen strangely marked birds and not-white flowers in the woods, and blood from cuts, but they had no vocabulary to describe the colors. Even the word "color" was forbidden. Here before them, plain to see, were greens and yellows and reds and purple and grays and blues and pinks. Unheard of. Unbelievable. Indescribable. The colors assaulted and excited them. It was as if they were hearing music after not having heard music before, as if they had not known of oceans before seeing one.

The Demo to whom the Presbyter had entrusted a package given him by the Adelphos, handed it back to the Presbyter. He opened it. It was yellow. It was cloth. But though he turned in this way and that, he had no idea what it was. "Here," said Sophia the Wise. "Give it to me." It was a robe. She placed it on the Presbyter's shoulders.

"Oh, oh," said the Phosphoros again and again. "Oh, just look at that." They inspected the Presbyter, elegant with the golden cloth against his whiteness. They lost any timidity and crowded up against him, touching the cloth. They turned to the tawny Demos and inspected them in their beautiful clothing. Shyly they touched their clothes. Carefully they patted the arms of the Demos.

Then, at a signal, the Demos reached into their pockets and pulled out swatches of colored cloths, the greens and reds and all the others, and handed them to the Phosphoros, who, young and old, shrieked with pleasure. They waved them in the air. They held them against their bodies. They smelled them; they tasted them. They begged for more and more of the cloth, as if for candy.

The children threw them into the air, and watched the colors sail against the sky. Some fixed them on sticks and paraded their banners through the crowd.

But, a terrible, angry voice interrupted the festivity. "What is all this?" demanded a deep, fearsome noise. "How dare you play with these heretical items? Take them off! Throw them on the ground. Trample on them. Spit on them. Drop them. Go home. Right now. DO YOU HEAR ME?"

It was the Archon who had emerged from the holy Archonery. Though he walked uncertainly, resting his weight on two soldiers, his voice roared. He railed as he walked, "Get rid of that trash." As he neared the group he snatched at the colored swatches and threw the leprous material on the ground. Hatred of all he saw emanated from his eyes, his mouth. "How dare you? Just how dare you?" As he turned to the yellow-covered Presbyter, many retrieved their cloths. "You! You are behind this.

You are finished. Now take off that horrible rag and throw it on the ground. Someone bring fire. Now! Burn this pestilence."

But, there arose a moaning, swelling from the Phosphoros. "No," they murmured, "No. No. No." The Presbyter looked around him. The Phosphoros were clutching their bright cloths. Some held them behind them. Some began to edge away. The Presbyter smiled. The moaning swelled. "No. No. No."

His face reddening, his green eyes bursting, the Archon said. "Obey, fools, Obey! You will ruin everything!"

Taking the feeble Archon firmly by the arm, the Presbyter said, "Honorable Archon, listen to me. We will not give up these slight treasures which have just now been given us by our friends, the Demos." The Archon's eyes squinched. His mouth twisted, teeth ready to bite. He snarled. The Presbyter continued unperturbed, "New life has come to us. White is death. Color is life. Look how we love these beautiful colors. We have new friends. They've given us these colors. This is indeed life. We have much to learn from them." He paused. "And, you, Mighty Archon, you will participate with us or you are finished." There was a low chorus of agreement. From far back in the crowd, one of the Phosphoros shouted agreement. Others joined in and the chorus grew bolder and bolder. "Go home, O Archon," said the Presbyter. "Now."

For the Archon, this was the apocalypse. Stunned by scorn for his sacredness, he collapsed into the arms of his soldiers, who, on orders from the Presbyter, half-walked, half-carried him to the Archonery. The assembly – the Phosphoros and the Demos, the Presbyter and Sophia and Demi – silently watched as the Archon entered the Archonery. They watched as the door slowly closed. Then the giggling and grinning and chattering revived. Waving their treasured swatches, as if for conquering heroes, the Phosphoros sauntered giddily toward their houses. And because it was growing dark, a few moments later, children came back into their yards, still carrying their colorful cloths, and began to light the fraxinella bushes in front of their houses.

Soon it was quiet in the square. Demi, the Presbyter, Sophia and the Demos looked about them. The Presbyter said, "This is enough for one day, don't you agree?" There was no dissent. "May I suggest that you five go home now, and that tomorrow at mid-morning all of you return with another five of your brothers and sisters. We don't want to overwhelm the Phosphoros with too many visitors. Tomorrow we'll truly begin a new life in this village. We have much to learn from you. And I promise you," he said looking directly at the Demos, "that tomorrow we'll also begin to remove the bodies of your fallen brothers from the pit where they lie so they can be taken up the mountain and honored among your people."

At mid-day the next morning the village people turned and stared at the side of their valley where the path led up to the crest, the home of the Demos. What drew their attention was the faint sound of singing, which drew them away from whatever occupied them. They walked quickly to the spot where the path began. The sound of the singing increased, and before long the Phosphoros could see colors through the trees. So it was that the Demos emerged singing and waving bright banners: striped and cross-hatched, rectangular and round, tri-angled and pin-striped. Gold and silver, blues and oranges, black and white, variations without end. Some carried large bolts of white sheets.

They sang as they entered the village and marched in playful formations. They ended their display with "Good morning, Dear Neighbors!"

"Good morning to you, Dear Neighbors," answered the Phosphoros enthusiastically.

Demi and Sophia stood back to watch as life unfolded. Eulie circled and cart-wheeled above, while Cynique stood sedately by Sophia's side.

The Presbyter came forward. "Greetings and welcome, dear Demos friends. Welcome back to you five who were here yesterday and welcome to you five who are here for the first time. This is a moment of beginning for all of us. This is the beginning of new life.

"We will come to know one another. We will exchange ideas and customs, and we will grow. About that we will speak more later. Right now we have urgent business." The Presbyter addressed the villagers. "Let me explain our urgent business. Many of you do not know that there have been occasions over many years when the Demos have sent emissaries, that they have been maltreated. Many have died at our hands."

There was a murmur in the crowd, some cries of disbelief. The eyes of some darted about and finally looked at the ground. "I fear," said the Presbyter, "that it is true. I have been involved, too. But all that will change as of now. We have nothing to fear. Many thought they needed to fear the Demos. But no more do we think so. Instead of fear we now have life." The Phosphoros stood silently, most trying to grasp just what the Presbyter meant, though some understood perfectly well.

The Presbyter continued. "Some thirty or forty Demos have died at our hands."

"Forty-three," said one of the Demos.

"Yes. Forty-three," said another.

"So, today we shall begin to right a wrong in small measure by seeing that the bodies of those who have died are returned to their people."

He turned to the mirrorman and the spearman. "Go to the Archonery and bring back all those poles, those staves that lean up against the wall. Fear not for the Archon. He will say nothing. He has taken to his bed. He is not well."

When they had gone, the Presbyter said to the Demos, "Have you brought that white material? Is it what I think it is for?"

"Yes, we have. Yes," they said quietly.

When the two soldiers returned with the poles, the Presbyter selected ten of the Phosphoros he knew to have been active in the night hunts, and they and the ten Demos and Sophia and Demi, and Eulie and Cynique, began the long walk into the forest beyond the village.

When they reached the sinkhole, the whole company gazed at the contents. The Demos were overcome at the sight, at the disgrace with which their fellows, their brothers and fathers, their uncles and sons had been treated. Some fell to their knees. Some of the Phosphoros covered their eyes with their hands.

"You see what we have done," said the Presbyter, to no one in particular. "But, we *will* make amends. It will be our work to bring the bodies out, and prepare them to be carried home." He ordered the mirrorman and the spearman to climb down into the pit. He instructed the Demos to take their white cloth and prepare slings from it with which to bring the bodies out. The cloth was cut and lowered into the pit. "Gently, gently," ordered the Presbyter. The soldiers gingerly placed a body into the sling and it was gently lifted out of the pit.

"Now take the poles, and wrap the sling sheet around the poles and place the body between the poles so that it forms a litter." He spoke softly. "Cover the body." And it was done.

Soon there were ten litters ready. With a Phosphoro and a Demo on each end, the group walked back into the village bearing the litters. At the village they rested, and then began their trek up the mountain.

To the surprise of all, another group of Demos came down the hillside and into the village in the middle of the afternoon. They carried large beautiful woven baskets and pottery vessels, filled with colorful items. The Phosphoros cautiously edged forward.

Smiling, the visiting Demos signaled that the villagers should come close. The Demos laughed as they took from their vessels fruits and vegetables, reds and yellows and greens and blues and whites and blacks and purples. They took knives and cut some of them and placed bits of them in their mouths and invited the Phosphoros to taste them also. Again with caution, some of the braver dared to taste, and they shyly approved.

One of the Demos reached into another basket and removed some sealed jars. He opened them, and took a brush from the basket and walked to a nearby house and dipped his brush into a jar and coated the frame of one of the windows of the house blue. There was astonishment from the onlookers. A boy said, "Let me do it!"

So, it came to pass that the Phosphoros became acquainted with colors: colorful clothing, colorful food, colorful paints. Their conversion to color was instant. They immediately invented names for these colors: sky and sunset and leaf and mouth and bruise and town and dawn and cloud and night.

After observing these goings-on, Demi said "We must go. Now!" Her voice trembled. "We're through here. We must find Uncle Theo so we can find Cora. We must go now. Let's leave."

"Good. We can just leave. All is well," said Sophia. Then she felt the press of the golden ball in her pocket. "What about the ball, Demi? Is there anyone fair here? It is inscribed 'for the fairest'."

"Yes, there are many fair-skinned here, but no one deserving of the ball. We must continue. We must find Theo."

"Which way shall we go?" asked Sophia.

They looked around, judging the landscape, and it seemed natural to them to turn toward the end of the village which they had first entered. As they walked that way, Sophia's eyes were drawn upward.

"Look, Demi, there are three moons. Three full moons. Look! Amazing. In a row! What a wonderful sign. I love moons." Demi saw them, too, and though little moved her, she gasped.

Sudden laughter from the village caused them to stop and look back. Then, when they looked up at the three moons, they were gone. Uncle Theo was at work. Demi and Sophia, and Eulie and Cynique followed the trail of the vanished moons.

Peripatetics

As they entered the frost-glazed forest at the perimeter of the village of the Phosphoros the drum beat began again, now insistently. At the edge, even the forest floor had been cleansed of fallen branches and brush and was coated with white. "It's their holy security," said Sophia disdainfully. Quickly they passed through this unnaturalness and were in true woods – woods of browns and blacks and grays and rainbows of greens.

It was a forest of sycamores and acacias, of eucalyptus and pistachios, a forest such as a forest should be – in orderly chaos, living and dying, and dying and living. Demi and Sophia pulled their cloaks about them in the deepening shade. Their path became a track. Branches and bushes pulled at them, defending themselves against interlopers. Demi said, "This is irritating. We are being impeded and impelled. Send Eulie ahead to scout for us."

"Eulie," Sophia said, "follow the path. See where it goes." Eulie spiraled himself high above them, rejoicing in the pull of his wings, and was gone. The others pushed on and came to a clearing.

Because the day was drawing to an end, they decided to spend the night. Sophia and Demi picked mountains of cynthian leaves for their beds and lay down. Sophia searched her pockets unsuccessfully for scraps of food. Demi likewise searched fruitlessly. They lay on the leaves and pretended they did not care about food. Cynique searched, successfully.

They slept, but at midnight Sophia wakened. She and Cynique walked the trail. There was a moon. She rejoiced to see it, though it only appeared through the trees. They heard faint rustlings in the woods beside them, the whish of wings in the air, and the subtle whisper of a snake's skin against the grass.

Eulie appeared and startled Sophia by landing on her shoulder.

"What have you to report?" Sophia asked.

"The sea and a village. Both not far."

"Are you sure? The sea *and* a village? This is not one of Theo's tricks?"

"No, it's real."

"Not another village. Is it white?"

"Yes."

"Oh, no. Not again. Is it far?"

"A few hours' march, considering the challenges of the trail."

"Is there food there?"

"Yes," said Eulie. "Fine village. I looked about in it. Interesting. Fruit trees along the way."

"I will need more than fruit," said Sophia. "It might not agree with my stomach."

In the morning, as Demi wakened, Sophia told her what Eulie had reported about the sea and the village. "Is this another of a Theo's tricks?" asked Demi.

Eulie answered, "No."

"We will see. We will see. And if it is a trick, Eulie, I will wring your neck." They walked on.

Soon the character of the forest began to change. Now there were cedars and cypress, cherries and wild olives. Through the groves they increasingly heard a roaring and crashing. "The sea!" Sophia said.

Cynique dashed ahead, and came running back. Yes, it was the sea. They hurried along and stopped at the edge of a precipice. Below lay the sea, its waves battering endlessly at house-sized boulders.

Cynique, who had never seen the sea before, leaped onto one of the massive stones below to investigate. A rogue wave fell on him and took him captive. He foundered, interred at sea.

Sophia cried, "Cynique! Cynique!" but before she could yell again, a whale-wave lifted him up and spit him out, dumping him on Sophia. Sophia squeezed the sodden dog over and over, hoping for life.

He suddenly belched out water, shook himself regally and stood, as if to say, "See? Nothing can hurt me." Sophia, wave-soaked and dog-sodden, regretted her compassion.

Their distraction with the sea and Cynique meant that they had not noticed the walled village perched on a hill well to their left. "Look," said Demi, "just as Eulie predicted." She looked again, and added, "Oh, no. Not another white town!" The beat became demanding.

The buildings against the sky-blue sea from this distance were indeed white, but they also were trimmed colorfully around the doors and windows.

"How far away is this town?" asked Demi.

Eulie said, "1810 meters."

"That's 1810.5 meters," corrected Sophia

"Well, if we want to get there, and I do very much," said Demi, "we have no recourse but to go back the way we came. There's no shore to follow. We can't get to that village from here." When they turned back, they found the cedars had filled in where once the path had been. "Damn and hell! This has to be the most elaborate of Theo's tricks yet. Come, Sophia, we'll force our way. Let's go."

They stood side by side, filled their lungs, and began to blow. A river of wind flowed out of them. Not a lily-livered zephyr, but a cyclone, a borean storm, spewed forth from the two, and the cedars bent and cracked.

As surely as the judges fell back on their chairs, as surely as the Archon and his henchmen dropped in heaps, as easily as the Red Sea parted before a strong east wind, so the psalmic cedars snapped and popped and fell to left and to right. Blowing gales, the two strode along the path, stopping finally at the glade where they had spent the night. There they calmed down, and they rested.

When at long last they glanced back at the path they had stormed, they had a surprise. The cedars were gone. Gone. Even they, sophisticated as they were, were unprepared for what they saw. In the place of the ravaged cedars was a great, open grove of olive trees. Through the trees they could see the ocean. They even thought they could just catch a slight glimpse of the town.

Demi said, "Our dear Uncle Theo is becoming more devious." She paused, adding, "But, Eulie's neck is safe, since the sea and the town are not a trick. Sophia, I surely hope that Theo is nearby. We'll find him and then be able to get to Cora. I feel giddy." They had overcome the trick. "You know, it wasn't really so hard," she said. "And look, are those ripe olives? I could stand something to eat."

Sophia said, "Have you ever eaten an olive right off the tree? You would regret it."

"Of course. Yes. Of course. I am well aware of that." She looked desperately for distraction. "Oh," she said, "Is that a path over there? It might be going in the direction we want to go. And look, the pistachios are ready to eat. That will help."

Off they went, in a direction that seemed likely to lead towards the shining town. Demi and Sophia gathered handfuls of pistachios and stuffed them in their pockets and chewed on them as they went, spitting out the hulls. They were raw, but edible.

The path led them through a bower. Underfoot lay a carpet of tiny blue-petaled acmes. Overhead, isthmian vines dripping with orangish aesops twisted thickly and darkened the trail so that, as it is more or less written elsewhere, "the sun could not have struck them by day nor the moon by night." But soon they were out in the bright, and there before them lay the town.

CALLOPOLIS

The high-walled town perched well above the bay. Its walls prevented even the most furious of waves from breaching them, but were wide enough to allow the inhabitants to walk on them, to enjoy the sea in all weathers and in all seasons.

As the four – Demi, Sophia, Cynique and Eulie – approached the village they were struck by its clean lines, by its curves and the bends of its buildings.

"Do you smell what I smell?" asked Demi.

"What? What do you smell? I don't smell anything but flowers," said Sophia.

"Exactly," said Demi. "How refreshing to approach civilization and not smell its debris, its unpleasant outpourings."

"Oh, Demi," said Sophia, "You are so polite. You mean we can't smell the smells of burning garbage and human waste. There. I said it. And you're right. There's a purity to the air. Amazing."

Their path joined a road leading to the village, which ended at a gated door to the town. They knocked several times, until the door swung open.

A pleasant young woman said, "Welcome to Callopolis, our Beautiful City. It's a beautiful day and it is beautiful to have you here. Welcome! Welcome to our beautiful city. Welcome to Callopolis. Please come in."

She continued, "I should tell you that my name is Alexandra, and I am the doorkeeper and guide here. May I ask your names?"

"Yes. Certainly. My name is Demi and this is my daughter Sophia, and this bird is Eulie and that sweet dog there is called Cynique."

"Once again, welcome to you all to this beautiful city, Demi and Sophia and Eulie and Cynique. I want to explain that the purpose of Callopolis, the beautiful city, is the perpetual promotion of beauty. Can you imagine living in beauty and having it as your purpose in life? It is simply wonderful. Now, let me give you a little tour of our fair city."

"Excuse me, Alexandra," said Sophia. "Is there a chance that we could find something to eat? We haven't eaten for a very long time. I am speaking of Demi and myself. These two," she said pointing over her shoulder to their animals, "have taken care of themselves. I think I see a bit of a mouse's tail sticking out of Eulie's beak. He chews on it as if he had a cud."

Alexandra immediately took them to a restaurant where they dined on panpipe pears, sweet aegyptian greens and cylindrical bass. A waiter brought an ovidian nut cake for dessert, but both declined. Enough nuts for one day.

Then Demi said sharply, "Let's go! We can't dawdle. We're looking for my young daughter."

"Oh," said Alexandra. "What's her name? Perhaps she is here? Is she beautiful? If she is beautiful perhaps she is here."

"Her name's Cora, and it is doubtful that she's here, though she is beautiful," said Demi. "But we'll keep an eye out as we walk through the town."

"Certainly, though over the years we've had many Coras here. None now that I know of. Let me explain something to you. As I said, the purpose of this town is to uphold and exalt beauty. Basically this means that the business of Callopolis is beauty. For us that means beauty contests. Nonstop beauty contests. Several a day. And they cover a massive range of the beauty. Here. They take place on the agora here."

Theo's Tricks / 133

If the drum beat had been insistent earlier, it gained force as they looked around. The agora, the town square, was filled with platforms of many sizes and heights, their dimensions depending on what was being judged. There was room for spectators at each stage, and a curtained off area for the contestants to wait.

Around the perimeter of the agora stood many shops, each aimed at the beauty market. One shop advertised: "Music Lessons: Calliope and Callasmaria teachers". Another said "Calisthenics by Philomena", which none too subtly assured contestants that strength could be beautiful. A shop operated by Agnes and Charis offered lessons in calligraphy for any who should care to write letters home, not to mention signing autographs.

Flower shops abounded, since some contestants liked to adorn themselves with flowers. A sign outside one shop read: "Phyllis and Chloe, Finest flowers", while a competitor who beckoned across the way was under the direction of Chloris, Iolanthe and Anthea.

Alexandra pointed across the square to a row of storefronts. "See over there? That group of shops is what we fondly call 'Teca Row'."

They walked past the Biblioteca and the books in the window promoting beauty enhancements. Next was a Discoteca. "For late-night fun for the beauties," explained Alexandra unnecessarily.

There followed next a Oenoteca. The labels of the bottles of wine in the windows featured shapely feminine figures. "They say," said Alexandra "that a swig or two on those wines will make you feel pretty, even if you aren't. Of course, they also say that if you feel pretty you will have an aura of prettiness about you that will overwhelm those near you."

They walked past other "tecas" and were on the verge of crossing the street when Demi's eye caught the name of another teca: "Theoteca". She grasped Alexandra's arm and said "What, what is this?"

"Oh, that," said Alexandra. "That's Uncle Theo's place. A sort of office."

"Uncle Theo?" said Demi and Sophia at the same time. "Uncle Theo?" both said, echoing one another. "Is he in there? We've been looking for him for a long time."

Alexandra peeked in the door, and said, "No. Not here. He keeps irregular office hours. He's out. Most likely he is not in town. He travels a good bit."

"What does he do in his office when he is there?" asked Sophia.

"What does he do? Oh, this and that. He counsels a few people. He issues summary judgments. And from what we can determine, he appears to delight in changing the lives of people who are unaware that their lives have been changed. They absolutely deny it. They say their lives are on the straight course they'd been planning all along, but we know better. We've heard that Uncle Theo calls it Mysterious Metamorphism. He smirks about his control."

Demi said, "Sounds like him. This is the closest we've come to finding Theo. I'm so happy that we got here. It does make me sure that Uncle Theo's been behind this all along. He may show up, you know. Let's keep a sharp eye out for him. We may have to stay here and wait for him. And of course he may be here in Callopolis right now. I'd sure love to get my hands on him.

"Now, Alexandra," Demi said, "let's keep walking so we can keep an eye out for Uncle Theo and you tell us about the contests." She could barely think with the noise of the drums.

"Gladly," she said. "Beauty has many aspects, as I'm sure you know. Let me see if I can explain. Generally, people look at the whole figure of a woman and her talents and then choose the best, or what they consider the most beautiful woman.

"Here in Callopolis we are completely unconcerned with any mental or physical talents our beauties have. For us it is all physical attributes. In this we follow the ancient dictum of the gods, particularly as endorsed by Uncle Theo – who established Callopolis, in case you didn't know it."

"Aha!" said Sophia, "So, just what is the dictum?"

"This is it, our guiding principle," said Alexandra:

Both beautiful and dumb,

my own true love must be.

Beautiful so I'll love her

and dumb so she'll love me.

"Oh," said Demi, "That is so heartwarming. It is the wisdom of the ages speaking. My heart is pounding."

"How capable you are of sarcasm, O Best Beloved Mother."

Alexandra, understanding none of these asides, said, "There is one important thing I want to tell you about the way Callopolis' contests work. Everybody is eventually a winner. If you lose an important pageant contest today, don't lose too much sleep, because eventually you'll win. Everybody gets a turn. You see we are deeply sensitive to self-esteem. We want no hurt feelings. No damaged egos around here. If you come out fourth or fifth, you need not fret. Somewhere down the line you will be the Gold Star winner and your feelings will send you to the moon in happiness. Isn't it a beautiful happy way of doing things? Self-esteem is everything."

The guide continued, "Now, back to the stages. I am sure you will find this interesting. For more years than anyone knows we have used the same stages for the same pageants, so that the beauty contestants can always find the correct platform. We don't want them to worry. No one should look dumb, even if they are dumb. And I should point out that each stage is dedicated to a specific contest. We do in fact judge various parts of the body. So, not to over-explain it overmuch, each platform is dedicated to a specific body part."

Alexandra paused for breath. "Now, for a slight retraction: I mentioned that different aspects of the figure are judged and that is the main emphasis here, but in fact there is one contest in which the whole body of a person is judged. It is The Callimorphos."

"Beautiful body. Beautiful shape," said Sophia, the pan-linguist.

"Indeed," said Alexandra. "You are impressive. We're not used to much intellectuality around here. Yes, here on this stage the whole body is judged."

"What's next?" asked Sophia.

"This next stage is the center of Callichiros." She paused, but there was no response. "Beautiful hands, anyone? All right, and over here is Callipodos."

"Yes," said Sophia. "Beautiful feet."

"We include legs here, too," added Alexandra.

"And this platform?' asked Demi, seeing one barely off the ground.

"This is a… how shall I put it? A popular contest spot. Here the Callimastos contests are held."

"I see," said Sophia. "That would be boobs."

"Yes, indeed. And as you indicate by your vernacular, the list of synonyms for *boobs* is exceedingly large. Because they come in so many sizes and shapes, divisions have long since been created in the Callimastos contests, which contestants can enter. For there's your large, your tiny, your round and so on. That makes it fair, don't you see, to be judged with your physical peers. You'll have to stop by and observe. I see on the sign board that the next contest is at noon. You owe it to yourself to make time, surely."

"Let's move on," came a voice.

"Yes, let's," said Alexandra. "I'm going to point out just a couple more, and let you wander around a bit and look at the others. Now over here is an interesting one. It's the site of the Callicephalos contests. You must know what that one is."

"Heads," said Sophia instantly, "beautiful heads."

"Of course. And you know how different they are. There are high foreheads and v-shaped jaws, and high cheekbones and the way teeth fit in a mouth makes a difference, doesn't it. The Callimeters have to take all these factors into account. Between us, there are those who think the Callimeters make their choices depending on how they happen to be feeling on any given day."

"Callimeters are judges of beauty," whispered Eulie into Cynique's ear. Cynique nuzzled up to Sophia's ears and passed the message on. Sophia wiped the remains of Cynique's affectionate message from her ear.

"Callimeters are judges of beauty," she said wisely.

"That's correct! Good for you," said Alexandra. "Oh, and here is one more place where the Callimeters work. This stage is dedicated to judging Callipugos."

There was a quizzical silence in the group. Each of the four looked at each other for enlightenment.

"Ah, then, friends," said Alexandra. "Here, on this spot, we judge beautiful bottoms. Beautiful rears. Beautiful butts, if you will. The *callipygian formation*, as it is frequently called. Callipugos are, as you know, as varied as the Callimastos. The Callimeters have a hard time deciding which is the best. Again, sometimes after an event we suspect that the Callimeters have been up too late the night before."

The silence of the four continued. Alexandra continued, "Do I detect that you are perhaps stunned? Well, it is a fact of life among us. Let me see. What else is there? Or perhaps you have some questions."

Silence again, then Demi spoke up. "As we have walked along here, we have seen women who I presume are the contestants. They are all young, aren't they?"

"Yes, normally they are between ages 14 and 22. Very, very occasionally there is a thirteen-year-old. Am I correct in thinking that you might be wondering where all these contestants come from?"

Heads nodded. "Well, twice a year there is a sort of fair that takes place and women come from all over the cosmos – do forgive the slight exaggeration – to see if they qualify. We have here what is called a Systematic Selection Scheme. It works quickly and efficiently and those who are not chosen are sent on their way with praises and wishes of good luck. It happens to them so quickly and efficiently they do not realize what has happened until much later. But they have had such a good time while they are here that we rarely hear of pouts or paroxysms."

"And," asked Demi, "What of those who stay? Do they stay beautiful forever? Do they not age? And if not, what happens to them?"

"Well," Alexandra paused. "Well," she paused again. "You know, Demi, no one has asked me that question before. I don't think it has ever occurred to anyone to ask. And I'm trying to think. Frankly, I don't know. But, now that you *do* make me think of it, I'm aware that sometimes people who have been around here for a while in the beauty game just seem to disappear. I have no idea where they go. Never thought about it. But, here's an idea," she said brightly, "if you ever run into Uncle Theo, ask him. After all, he is in charge. This is his place. This is his city. He must know where they all go."

Sophia became aware of the heavy gold ball in her pocket. "Demi," she whispered, "is there fairness here for fair ladies?"

"If you mean justice, I think not. But here we must be thinking of beauty. Fair beauty. The fairest. Otherwise why are we here? And how is it possible to judge which is the fairest?"

Sophia answered, "Judging who is the fairest among beauties? It's dangerous. It lets loose too many evils. It can cause wars. I'm done with this." She added, "What shall I do with the golden ball?'

"Keep it safe," said Demi. "We will surely find Uncle Theo and we can give it back to him. And good riddance. Let's keep walking." The drumbeat grew and grew and became polyrhythmic.

"Something is happening," said Demi.

They passed more platforms and stores. They saw crowds of beauties beginning to assemble at some stages. "Don't you want to stop and watch the activity?" asked Alexandra.

There were two strong "No's," and they kept on walking. As they neared a corner of the square, Sophia noticed a sign over a building which read "Hôtel Paris". Then she saw a man sitting on the veranda of the hotel surrounded by a score of beautiful women. Sophia grabbed Demi and said, "Look!"

"Oh," said Alexandra, "it's Uncle Theo!" And with a thunderous boom, the drumming came to an end. In the midst of Demi's and Sophia's exultant shouts of triumph, Alexandra added, "He's here, and I must point out that as usual he has some of yesterday's beauty winners with him."

On that day he had apparently chosen lean and thinly built redheaded women. Among those tangled around him were a copper-haired, thin-faced callicephalos, a slightly endowed but bosom-revealing callimastos with long geranium-tinted braids and the cherry-haired, bony-bottomed winner of a callipugos contest.

Uncle Theo, a short man of medium build, bearded, shirtless, grinning, was waving a bottle of wine. At almost the same time that they saw him, he saw Demi and Sophia and made a half-hearted move to disentangle himself from the gaggle of adoring redheads, who whined and pouted and protested his rising. They pulled at him to stay seated and, though he nearly succeeded in standing up, he gave up with a laugh and sat back down. "Welcome to Callopolis at last, my lovely relatives."

"Uncle Theo," said Demi. "We have certainly been looking for you."

Uncle Theo roared and said, "You certainly have, and how did you like the tricks? I enjoyed thinking them up. Oh, some of them were ingenious, didn't you think? I particularly liked the ice and debris crashing through the village of the Phosphoros. And I loved making the cavern of the Demos disappear from view. Oh, and the monopods on that trail. That was good. I have been near you most of the time, except at night when I had better things to do. You can see my motivation in coming to my beautiful village, my Callopolis."

He allowed himself to fold comfortably back into the eager arms of his willing and manifestly beautiful companions.

"Uncle Theo, this has indeed been a dreadful adventure. We demand that it be over. *Now*. We want to rescue Cora from DeVille *now*," said Demi. "We've ranged widely and we've been involved with more than our share of adventures. We've seen many species of humans and human behavior, not to mention this demeaning display in your fair Callopolis. For my part, I have had enough and want to get on with my life. So, could you please make it possible for us to rescue Cora? We have had enough of Fairness."

"Oh, yes indeed," said Uncle Theo, "However, I must say that your adventures have had some meaning for the most part. It was not all a loss. By the way, I'll take my sweet golden ball. I have lots of other plans for it, and the possibilities delight me."

Sophia handed the dull golden ball to Theo. "Good riddance."

"Thank you, sweet Sophia," he said. "And now, I too am busy, as you can see. I have many here to make happy, so it would be a good idea for you to go on your way." Uncle Theo continued, "Now. Tophat DeVille knows he must give up Cora to you. And you know how to get to The Necropolis. Plan to go.

"Next, as for returning to your village, here is what you do: retrace your steps. Go back through Callopolis the way you came in, follow the path back to the glade, and from there through the forest. You will come out by the village of the Phosphoros, but do not enter it. Life is carrying on very well. You did good work there. My compliments. Go back up the ridge the way you came, then down the other side, and pass by the Parliament of judges, which is still trying to recover from your recent visit. There may be one or two there who will think about your visit. Then you will pass by the trading post where you found the golden ball, and from there to your village. If you leave now you should arrive about sunset."

He added, "I know, I know, it does not seem possible. But trust me, you will get there today. When you arrive, you will find little activity because things have taken a backwards step since you left. Slowed down considerably, I would say. Do not concern yourselves. In the morning it will all be different. The sun will rise as is its custom. No one will remember what they have been through in this little while. It will be as if they had all sipped from the River Lethe."

Theo leaned back for a moment. Then, "Oh, there is one further thing. Do not go to The Necropolis until the morning of the third day after you arrive. It is important to let things settle down in the village. That's an order. Now, off with you. Nice to see you. Come again. Have a nice day."

The trip home was as Uncle Theo said. Demi, Sophia, Eulie and Cynique arrived in the dark, dreary fog in late afternoon. Demi went immediately to her house, and Sophia with Eulie and Cynique to her house across the way from Demi's. They each dined well and rested and reveled in blessed solitude.

In the morning the sun was shining. Yellowpants Hellerman was already at work when Demi wakened. School children inspected beetles on their way to school. Shopkeepers shouted at one another, and peddlers of frivolous merchandise were at work charming the birds from the trees. Someone called at Demi's door early to consult with her, as usual. It was another day.

Cycles

At long last it was the morning of the third day after they had arrived home. At first light Demi and Sophia left in Demi's coach for The Necropolis, stopping neither for food nor rest. They did not bother to mention their departure to anyone, for they expected to return before nightfall.

Demi, aching to see Cora, urged them along. She hoped she would not find Cora in hysterics. How Demi longed to cradle her sweet, weeping child in her arms and lovingly bear her home.

Yellowpants, of course, saw them tear off, and though he noted with scientific accuracy the details of their departure, he said nothing, and no one thought to ask him. It was all the same to him. After Demi and Sophia were no longer in sight, he turned his attention with equal interest to a cow in labor.

Sophia drove the horses. Demi sat beside her, holding on tight, in joyful anticipation. Cynique ran alongside the coach, and Eulie perched on Sophia's shoulder, enjoying the wind in his face.

It was not many hours before they came upon mobs of people on the roadway carrying their dead to The Necropolis. Sophia bullied the coach through the outer fringes of stretchers, drays, tilburies, dogcarts and travois, but soon they were so packed into the parade of the living and the dead that there was no room to maneuver.

They moved at the throng's dull pace. They yelled for the mob to make way. But they might as well have been speaking to the dead.

"Eulie," said Demi, "We're stuck! Fly up and see if there is anything we can do." Immediately the owl kited into the air and disappeared from view. Within moments he was back. He settled on Sophia's shoulder and hooted into her ear.

"Ah," said Sophia to Demi, "Eulie advises patience. He says before long we'll come upon a road which turns off to the left, and he says that if we follow it, we'll break free from this crowd and find another entrance to The Necropolis."

They plodded along fretfully until at last they reached a place where an unlikely, barely discernible track broke off. Eulie whispered assurances to Sophia, so they turned onto it. Demi and Sophia apprehensively followed the trail, bumping along, and leaving the crowd behind. But soon, very soon they passed through a gate and were inside the precincts of The Necropolis.

"Very good, Eulie! Very, very good, Eulie," Demi said, greatly relieved. Eulie preened and spun around twice on Sophia's shoulder.

As they continued, they realized that the hordes they had expected to see inside the grounds of The Necropolis apparently dispersed once they came through the gate, so that it was pleasantly uncrowded. Everywhere they looked, Demi and Sophia saw fields of yellow flowers dotted with monuments and statuary. People strolled about admiring the flowers and the delights of the cemetery.

Sophia pulled the coach onto a grassy spot and they alit. As they looked about they were filled with questions. What should they do now? Where should they go? How would they find Cora? Would Tophat appear and eject them from The Necropolis?

Demi saw a tall woman in red, who clearly was not connected with those delivering their beloved or not-so-beloved ones. Demi imperiously called out to her: "You, Red Dress, tell me, where can we find Cora?"

The woman in red turned and looked at them, her mouth dropping open. She stared at them. "Why," she said at length, "she's inside that building over there, playing hostess as usual. Go inside. You'll find her. And may I ask who you are?"

The building the woman had mentioned was in front of them, as plain as can be. Yet, because of their newness and perplexity, they had not been conscious of it.

Demi and Sophia, ignoring the woman's question, walked quickly toward the building, looking for an entrance. The woman in red, still with a surprised look on her face, scurried away. Demi and Sophia rounded the corner and found the entry. A large sign above the door said, "The Philadelphian Center Bids You Welcome!"

Once inside, they were surprised to be standing on a wide, sweeping balcony, overlooking a vast, crowded floor some distance below. At first, though they were aware of masses of people below, they were distracted by the building itself. Immense pillars supported the ceiling and provided ample space below for the movement of many people. The stone in the ceiling was brilliantly interlaced so it spanned the great space. The floor was interwoven with slabs of colorful marble.

Demi and Sophia turned to the crowds below. Their goal was to find Cora. Carefully they surveyed the people moving about.

Then Demi said, with some excitement, "Look, Sophia. See that young woman over there, almost in the center? She looks very much like Cora, but she's older, as if she were an older sister or a cousin."

"Oh, yes. I see her too. She does indeed resemble Cora to some degree, but she isn't Cora. She can't be. She's much older, considerably older." They searched through the crowds carefully for some time, yet their eyes would inevitably return to the young woman in the center. Demi and Sophia watched as people came up to her, apparently asking questions. She spoke with them briefly and they went off.

"She has a gracious way about her. Notice how she gives people motherly pats on the back," said Demi. "Let's go and talk to her. I don't see how she can possibly be Cora. Maybe she can tell us where to find her."

"Maybe, just maybe, she really *is* Cora. Maybe this is one of Theo's tricks," said Sophia. They walked down the broad staircase which led to the level where the crowds of people came and went.

They made their way through the crowd and stopped near the young woman. She was talking to someone when Demi said, "Hello," and the young woman turned and looked at her.

"Mother!" she cried out. "Mama!" She hurriedly turned back to the woman she had been talking with. Taking her by the arm she pointed her to a man with a green shirt.

"Cora?" said Demi and Sophia together.

"Yes, of course," said Cora. "Don't you know me? Your own daughter?"

"Yes, I suppose I do. Yes I do indeed," she said, and she and Cora embraced. Cora held her mother tightly and Demi breathed in her dear daughter.

"Hello," said Sophia over Demi's shoulder. She held out her hand.

"It's Sophia!" exclaimed Cora, and she gave Sophia as much of a hug as Sophia permitted. "What a surprise. I'm so happy to see you. I've waited such a long time," said Cora.

"Cora," said Sophia, staring closely at her sister, "You look so different. You are so changed. You look like a young woman to me. How can this be?"

"How can it be? What do you mean?" Cora asked.

"Well," said Sophia, "You have a young woman's look about you. When we last saw you, just a few days ago, you were a young girl. Now you have the figure of a woman. You have curves where you never were curved before. You are the perfect figure of a woman. You have a mature young woman's face."

Cora looked down at herself. She looked at her narrow waist, and ran her hands down the contours of her bosom and across the pleasant width of her hips. "I don't quite know what you are talking about exactly. I am what I am. And it certainly has not been just a few days.

"Let's not talk about that," said Cora. "Anyway, I'm so glad you are here. And I'm excited to show you this new building. It opened just a few days ago and it's my pride and joy since I designed it and oversaw its construction." Demi and Sophia looked at each other, eyebrows raised.

"You see, when I finished studying mathematics, I somehow stumbled onto the subject of architecture and read whatever I could lay my hands on. I had known that Tophat had felt for some time that it would be good to have a reception hall, so I designed this building and surprised him by proposing it to him. He amazed me because he liked it and had his engineers look it over. They made a few small corrections, but this building is my design." She paused to take it all in, and she smiled proudly.

"One of the features of this building, which is my pride and joy, is that system of interlocking blocks of marble in the ceiling. Look up there. Isn't it wonderful? See how they fit together and hold the ceiling up? That's Macedonian yellow marble up there. It helps make the building seem lighter, don't you think?"

Why is she talking so much about the building? Demi wondered.

"The columns are made of Aegean gray," Cora droned on, "not easy to get because of the limited amounts, but somehow Tophat laid his hands on enough. I suspect he twisted a few arms or paid somebody under the table for that gray," she said, laughing a little. "But money is no object."

Cora continued, not noticing her mother's face, a mass of confusion. "The walls are of Delphian white marble which contrasts nicely with the ceiling and the columns. Another of my favorites is the floor. Look here: these random shapes are of a marble called Ariadnian green. We had a marvelous workman cut the shapes which he then laid into this off-white marble from Naxos."

"Cora," interrupted Demi sternly, "We need to start for home."

"Home?" said Cora, "What do you mean? I *am* home." Ignoring Demi, she added, "But anyway, let me tell you what we do in this place. It's interesting and it's clever, and I want you to know all about it. Do you mind if I go on?" She smiled and did not wait for an answer.

Demi said firmly, "Now, Cora… " but Cora simply went on.

"I am sure you saw the name of this building when you came in. It is the Philadelphian Center. We chose that name on purpose because we wanted to give people a sense of cozy fellowship here. Isn't that a good idea? The people who come here have decisions to make about where to lay their friends and relations to rest. So we wanted to present a friendly atmosphere. We want them to have the impression that we care. But between you and me, it's all strictly business, of course.

"We guide people so they won't hesitate to make the right interment choices, and they go away satisfied with the burial arrangements. When they're finished with the arrangements, they often come back to people like me – the hosts and hostesses – or like that man over there in the green shirt, and tell us thank you. Lots of them are teary. I'm not entirely sure why, but it's my guess that they are emotional because people dear to them have died, and also because they have just made arrangements to have them buried in a beautiful spot. Maybe the tears are because they are satisfied. It's hard for me to tell. Oh, well, we see this all the time and we're used to it. Their tears really don't touch us.

"As I said, this is business, after all," Cora added. "And we're terribly good at guiding them into making arrangements which will be profitable to us. You can imagine that there is no profit to speak of from those buried in all those wet sites underground. There are expenses in expanding below, of course, so those costs have to be off-set.

"Cora – that's so crass," said Sophia.

"No, no. Not crass. We're realistic," said Cora. "I spend a lot of time here guiding people to make the right decisions. I'm quite good at it. They see me as sympathetic and helpful. And I am sympathetic, to a degree, but you realize that we deal with hordes of people everyday, so there is by necessity a certain toughness to us. As I said, with us it's just…"

Demi's fury finally erupted. She broke in on Cora's chattering. "What do you mean when you say 'I *am* home'? This certainly is not your home. You were kidnapped a few days ago and brought here against your will by Tophat. Your home is with us in our house in the village and with your friends."

"Mother! Demi! Please. My home is here."

"Cora! Cora!" shouted Demi.

Sophia quickly followed suit, echoing "Cora! Cora!"

At that moment Demi raised herself up into her full dominant being, reached out, and placed her hands defiantly down on Cora's shoulders.

Cora looked Demi straight in the eyes and said with slow and cool seriousness, "Please remove your hands from my shoulders this instant, Demi. You do not give orders here. This is my place. I give the orders here. I'm in charge here. You are not. All the people working here helping the mourners are under my charge. Let me repeat: I am in charge here, in every sense."

Cora's straight-eyed nerve startled Demi. Her hands dropped to her sides and, slumping down, she complied.

Cora glanced over Demi's shoulder, as if looking for something, and said, "Come with me. Follow me. Now." She led them across the vast space and into a small room. "Go inside."

She called out to the woman in red, who had been standing nearby watching them. "Rhoda, have someone bring us some food and drink. This is my mother and my sister, and they've traveled a long way and have had no food."

Rhoda said, "Yes, Cora. I'll take care of it for you. I've some things just out of the oven. I'll be back shortly. Please excuse me."

In the small room Demi and Sophia sat in comfortable chairs, with a low table before them. Cora closed the door and sat down. Leaning forward, she said, "I vaguely remember the time, a very long time ago, when I was taken from home. I don't remember the details of the actual incident because I was apparently given a potion of some sort and slept all the way here. When I woke up in a strange place, I was frightened. Very frightened. But I slowly began to be aware that the room I was in was actually a pleasant room. I was being watched over by someone who then turned out to be a very nice woman, though I thought of her as a captor at first. I soon met other nice women who became friends.

"One of these women, who I hope you will meet, made me quite angry by saying that I was a spoiled, indulged brat. I hated her for saying that."

"I should hope so," said Sophia, who was leaping ahead to where this story was going.

"But," Cora continued. "*But*... her name is Xantippe, by the way. As it turned out, despite the fact that Xantippe had a low opinion of me at first, she said she saw an inkling of potential and she encouraged me to begin learning. She was right. I had been a completely spoiled ignoramus. First she taught me to bake and cook and sew, which I found I quite liked. Xantippe showed me that in order to sew and bake and cook I had to use numbers and measurement. She taught me about numbers.

"When I began to find numbers interesting, she started me on mathematics. Mathematics means learning, after all, and from there to learning all sorts of things.

"One thing led to another. I already told you how math led to architecture. Then there were astronomy and physics and geology and biology. You know what I mean."

Demi's jaw dropped as Cora talked. It finally reached its limit.

"Oh, yes and art and music and rhetoric, and idiomatic philology. As far as literature goes, my favorite is drama and anything to do with theater. I might add I am a polyglot, and I am still working on new languages. Did I mention orthography and glossaries? It turns out that I am a polymath."

Cora saw that Sophia was yawning during this recital of her accomplishments. "Sophia, do you see what all this means?"

"Yes. You are not the same person that you were a little while ago," Sophia replied, then decided to test her. "Tell me about the effect of the moon."

After Cora lectured her briefly on physics and gravity, Sophia replied, "I see," though she had been thinking of the effect of moonbeams on her psyche.

"But, I still want you to come home. You are my little girl," said Demi.

"Dear Mother, how often do I have to explain that I *am* home? I can't think of living anywhere else. I'm quite happy here."

At that moment Rhoda knocked on the door gently and entered with a tray of food. The smells of warm goodness filled the room. Because of her training in self-effacing courtesy, Demi protested that she was not hungry, but the sight and smells of the food overcame her and she picked up a piece of fresh corinthian bread and spread demotic honey on it and devoured it. Sophia followed her example.

"Now, let me tell you about Tophat," said Cora, courteously declining to eat. "I know you don't like him, Demi, even though he is your brother. But I know him well. When it comes to acquiring wealth, he is ruthless, to put it mildly. And in his search for the company of women, he is rapacious. I was hardly the first person he stole away and brought here.

"All of the women I first met when I first arrived – Rhoda and Melantha and Xantippe, and my friends Sian and Chloris – were taken by him by one means or another, and brought to The Necropolis to serve his needs. That was his purpose in bringing me. He has told me many times how long he had admired me, and how he'd lusted after me even when I was young. Some people are like that, aren't they? I wanted nothing to do with him. Well, how would you feel?

"All my friends protected me for a long time; they saw to my education. I'd learned enough to evade Tophat, because my friends warned me that Tophat was after me. My friends would hide me or protect me from him, especially during his nightly forays."

As Cora talked, Demi squirmed. How could she believe the tale that her daughter was telling? Her innocent little daughter!

"Meantime, time passed, and I was, of course, changing, physically, I mean, though I had no idea about it because it is so gradual. All I knew is that Xantippe and others from time to time would tell me I needed better-fitting clothing. So, I became aware of my bumps and curves."

Demi gasped. *How could this be? This metamorphosis?*

"So anyway, Tophat was determined, and he saw I was often sharp with him. As I said, my education enabled me to defend myself, so he had no recourse but to be nice. He knew he was not going to take me by force. My friends assured me that not getting his way was quite comical. So he wooed me in a variety of ways, with rides and gifts and so on. In the end I was forced to be more or less *nice* to him."

Demi felt herself almost rise and heard herself say, "Listen here, now, child! I am your mother and you are going to listen to me." But in truth, though her body made slight gestures in that direction, she could not muster the strength. She simply sat, transfixed, asking herself, *how could our roles have reversed? How can she be in charge?*

All I want is to take her to her real home! If she were at home with me, she'd be her sweet old self… a fifteen-year-old, innocent of the world, except, of course, for those giggling friends of hers.

Demi, half-listening, began scheming. *Perhaps Sophia and I could persuade Cora to come outside the building where we could somehow overtake her and put her in the coach. We would have to tie her up. How would we keep her from protesting?* She glanced at Sophia and noted the sash she was wearing. *That would do nicely.* She looked around the room, but it was bare of anything useful for abduction. What to do?

Cora's voice broke through to Demi, when she said "…my first night with Tophat… "

The words jarred Demi, bringing her back to the moment. She yelped, "What did you just say? With Tophat – my brother?"

Cora smiled and said, "Haven't you been listening to me, Demi?"

"What is it that you just said about Tophat? My mind was wandering."

"Really, Demi. I have been talking about him for the last ten minutes, and… isn't that right, Sophia?" Sophia nodded. "I was just about to tell you about the first time I spent the night with Tophat. You know… how it happened and what happened." Cora continued, "What ever have you been doing, Demi? Dreaming? I'd have thought you'd be paying attention. Please do not be upset. This is just a business arrangement I have with Tophat. There is no love here."

"'*Business*?' Business? Honestly, child, Now I am more convinced than ever that I must take you home. Wouldn't you come for a visit?"

"Demi!" said Sophia, "Don't you want to hear the rest of Cora's story?"

"Cora," asked Demi, "Would you consider coming home for a visit?"

"Let's hear the rest of her story, *please!*" Sophia pleaded.

"Sophia, please," Demi demanded. "I know that you're perfectly capable of filling me in with all the details. Cora has no need of going on. Now, please, Sophia, I'm trying to talk to Cora." Sophia sulked and turned her back on them.

"Cora, what do you say? Come home for a short visit? Please."

Cora looked at her mother for a long time, and then said, "I admit that it sounds inviting." After a pause, she said, "I think I *will* go with you for a visit."

Demi smiled and a little shriek of joy almost escaped her, but didn't, because she was suddenly taken aback at seeing Cora staring at her, unflinching, expressionless. This frightened Demi, causing her to wonder what the staring meant. Sophia, mouth agape, was also drawn to Cora's impassive face, but it was her guess that Cora was not so much staring as she was thinking intently about a visit. Sophia was right.

Cora finally said, "About making the visit, I realize I need to consult with Tophat about it. I'll let you know. So, I'll leave you right now." She arose, started for the door, then turned and said sternly, "Do not leave this room. Don't even open the door. Stay here. You will be comfortable. Everything you need is here, and I'll have Rhoda look after you. I don't know how long I'll be away. But no matter, do not leave this room. That's an order." And she walked out the door without looking back.

Demi and Sophia stared at Cora's back as she left. They watched her cross the floor and walk up the grand staircase, and then they lost sight of her. Rhoda said from the door. "I'll be back before long." She too disappeared.

They sat back in their chairs and tried to rest, though both were too agitated to settle down. Gradually the room darkened and their eyes grew heavy. They were almost asleep when Rhoda came into the room with a tray of food. She walked quietly when she saw that the two were so relaxed. A little bump of her foot jarred them. "I have warm food for you," she said.

They had hardly begun to eat when Cora returned. "It is all arranged," she said. "Let's go to my apartment. You can spend the night there and we'll leave in the morning. Your carriage is under shelter and the horses – and the dog also."

"His name is Cynique," sniffed Sophia. "Eulie can fend for himself."

Cora said to Rhoda, "Bring the food and they can eat in my apartment." Turning to Demi and Sophia, Cora said, "Follow me."

Cora turned to the door, and waited. "Well? Shall we go?" When she walked out of the door, Sophia and Demi collected themselves and hurried along. Cora was by that time near the stairway. At the top, Cora paused, looking back. The moment Demi and Sophia stepped onto the balcony Cora was out the door and walking swiftly across a grassy field, and then into a large building. She waited at the doorway, and gestured that they were to follow her. She led them down corridors and through passageways and across two courtyards, and finally paused at a door. "This is my apartment. You're welcome to spend the night here."

Again she said, "Make yourselves at home. I will not be here. I will be with Tophat tonight." Then she left.

Demi and Sophia were stunned. It was as if a hangman had walked briskly up the steps to a platform, had made short work of his business, and gone on to his next appointment.

Rhoda followed carrying the food and set it on a table. Demi and Sophia still stood near the door and looked around them. If this was the room Cora had mentioned being in when she first arrived at The Necropolis, it was indeed a very nice room. "See the paintings," said Sophia. There was the pastoral scene with the little girls, and the one with the sphinx and the pearl, and others.

"Come eat," said Rhoda. "I believe that some of Cora's friends are coming to meet you. They're curious about you."

An hour later Xantippe, and Melantha, and Sian and Chloris all came to the apartment to have a look at the visitors. Nothing was particularly novel about Demi and Sophia, so they began to tell stories about Cora — about what a naïve, innocent, ignorant child she had been; about how, somehow, a spark had been lit within her so that she began to learn and to take interest in learning — on and on they went, about how she had been able to handle Tophat, not to mention another gentleman who used to appear from time to time. How she managed them. Both of them.

Xantippe and Rhoda and Cian and Chloris and Melantha also expressed their amazement that Cora had matured and had become what she was, a multi-talented, vibrant young woman.

The door opened and Cora entered. She looked at the scene and said to Demi and Sophia, "Well, you appear to have been having a jolly time. You have some curiosity-seekers here. Don't worry, they're my friends and they're harmless.

"Demi, we'll be leaving early tomorrow morning, so I suggest you get some rest. And you," she addressed the other women, "all of you, scat!"

In the morning Cora came for Demi and Sophia. "The carriage is ready. We can leave any time."

Demi asked, "Is everything set with Tophat?"

"Yes, perfectly."

Sophia asked, "What did he do when you told him you were going?"

"He said he knew I would be going, but he didn't know just when. So, in a way, he was prepared. This morning he embraced me, and held my head tenderly with his hands, and put his forehead on my forehead, and he whispered something that I did not quite understand. He also presented me with some exotic seeds to eat — seeds he said he had just found in his travels. I found them tasty, although they gave me a delightfully strange sensation. Shall we go? The carriage is waiting."

They began their journey, expecting to arrive by nightfall. Cynique trotted alongside happily, allowing himself occasionally to flush a bird. Eulie, elated to be going home, pirouetted and tumbled high above them.

As they traveled, Cora fell asleep, and Demi put her arms around her and held her closely. Her eyes feasted on her beloved daughter. Yet something began to happen to Cora. She began to shrink, as it were, to lose weight, to change her appearance. Her clothing became bulky. And before they had gone far, Sophia and Demi saw their beloved fifteen-year-old child there before them, leaning up against her mother.

Demi and Sophia kept silent and looked at each other in wonderment at this transformation. Still, they admitted to each other later, knowing their experiences with Uncle Theo, they were only partly amazed.

When they arrived home, Cora awoke and looked out the windows of the coach. "What a sleep I have had."

"Yes, indeed," said Sophia. They walked with Cora, still heavy-eyed, into the house and led her to her room. They removed her clothing, and hung them all in a closet, and dressed her in new robes.

In the morning Cora slept late. She wakened and called out, demanding food. Later on, a maid came and they played at choosing her clothing for the day. She and the maid read some stories of little animals, and then her friends arrived. They gossiped and squealed and walked in the village. They all returned to Cora's house and had supper together.

Thus many happy months passed.

Early one morning, just as Cora was waking, she distinctly sensed an odd noise. As she tried to work out what it was, she began to think perhaps she was hearing the sounds of a rolling carriage and of horses' hooves. She straightened up so she could listen more intently.

What was it? She went to the window. From there she heard the rumble of the village shopkeepers calling their wares. She heard the shouts of children running and tripping on their way to school, the squeal of oil-less wagon wheels, and the teasing of milkmaids on their way to their cows. Yet through it all she was increasingly aware of what might be the sound of a carriage.

With a burst of light, an epiphany, a shattering trumpet, Cora knew. She gasped. A picture of Tophat burst upon her. She could see him holding her head gently in his hands, and she could taste the exotic seeds. She knew.

She rushed to the closet, found the old clothing, and ran barefoot out of the house in her nightgown, carrying the clothes over her shoulder.

She hurried to the field, over to the rising where the exotic flowers grew, and down to the road below where a black carriage and four horses stood waiting. She stopped to snap off a double-headed daffodil before she climbed into the carriage and gave Tophat DeVille a kiss on the cheek. Tophat tapped the roof of the carriage with his cane and called, "To The Necropolis, as fast as you can."

As they rode, Cora tore off her nightgown and put on the old clothing, which, before many miles fit her nicely. Tophat threw Cora's nightgown out the window.

One of the maids quickly reported to Demi that Cora was not to be found. They searched the house and the village. Demi, realizing she had been foolishly wasting time, ran to the Great Dendron Tree. "Yellowpants! Yellowpants" she called, and was answered with a grumbling from above.

"I am busy. Come back tomorrow."

"No, Yellowpants. I won't. You must tell me if you saw Cora leave this morning."

"You will have to wait. I am busy watching a fox sneak up on the sheep while the shepherd's back is turned. I am also watching the beginning of rain coming from the north. It will be heavy, but there you are."

"Yellowpants, if you do not answer me, I will have this tree cut down and turned into firewood for the villagers before the day is out."

Yellowpants, grumbling and muttering about untoward, unprofessional interferences in his work, said, "Yes. I did see Cora. It was early this morning. She came running across the field with some clothing thrown over her shoulder. Oh-oh! The shepherd sees the fox. Now he is throwing a stone at him. There was a black carriage waiting there. She picked a flower and got in. It was the same carriage as the one that passed by a few days ago. That's all I know."

Demi felt ill.

This was to be only the first of these instances in uncountable years ahead. It was the first of many times that this elaborate liturgy was played out.

Each time that Cora disappeared, Demi and Sophia would wait a few months, then board their carriage and drive to The Necropolis. There, as usual they would find Cora at work in the Philadelphian Center, generously allowing people to spend money on elaborate graves. Demi and Sophia were always kindly persuasive, urging Cora to return for a short visit.

During the months when Cora was in the home of her mother, deeply involved in her normal routines, innocent of any other life, there always came that moment when unexpectedly she became aware of the sound of the carriage — while eating dinner with her chattering friends, or sometimes in the middle of the night, and sometimes when the maid was entertaining her with adventure tales of wee animals. She would realize, as waking to reality from a fantasy, that she must get the clothing hanging in the closet and run determinedly across the field to the road where a carriage waited for her. Then her memory of life at home with Demi and Sophia and her friends would fade altogether.

Yellowpants saw all the disappearances except for those that occurred after dark. He was not much given to analysis, but he dimly recognized a pattern.

Thereafter, every time Cora disappeared, Demi would go first to Yellowpants to confirm a matter of the most searing importance to her. And every time, Yellowpants would fume and fuss about being interrupted for such trivial and ephemeral matters.

Mythological elements in *Theo's Tricks*

Persephone, who is kidnapped.
Demeter, who searches for her.
Hades, who takes Persephone for his wife.
Hecate, who loves the moon and trivia.
Helios, who sees all and tells reluctantly.
Midas, who has a problem with gold.
Uncle Theo? Who is Uncle Theo?
The golden ball, which is inscribed "For the fairest".

About the Author

William Tudor is a retired Episcopal minister who lives in the Pacific Northwest. During his years of active ministry, he and his family lived in the East and the Midwest, as well as in Medellín, Colombia (for seven years). His maternal grandfather and his mother were published writers. His brother Steve was a noted poet.

Bill's interest in Greek myths is long standing, but only lately has he delved more deeply into them. Aiding and abetting that interest is his love of words. During the writing of *Theo's Tricks*, that interest naturally turned to the Greek language, since there are countless English words of Greek origin. In writing *Theo's Tricks*, several hundred of these words found their way into the text.

His contact with Greek began in college, when he was required to learn the Greek alphabet, and developed in seminary, where he studied the Greek New Testament. He is far from expert, but he can puzzle out written Greek words a bit and is pretty sure he knows a Greek/English word when he sees one.

Made in the USA
Charleston, SC
15 September 2013